Y'ALL WANTED A KING

A BIBLICAL ROAST OF LEADERSHIP GONE WRONG AND THE GOD WHO FIXES IT

CARLA HENRY-LEWIS

Y'ALL WANTED A KING

A Biblical Roast of Leadership Gone Wrong and the God Who Fixes It

This book—and the Spiritual Makeover series—is dedicated to those who have been hurt by decisions made in the name of God that bore no resemblance to His character.

To everyone wounded by weaponized Christianity—by faith used to control, exclude, punish, or protect power—this series begins with acknowledgment.

As an African American, I know the familiar refrain: "We are not responsible for what our ancestors did." Yet healing has never required inherited guilt— only honest recognition and the courage to repair what remains broken.

So let this stand as recognition.

Cruelty has been committed in the name of Christianity.

Scripture has been twisted to justify injustice.

And many were harmed while others insisted God approved.

For that distortion, I am sorry.

Not for God—but for those who misrepresented Him.

The Spiritual Makeover series exists to do what surface faith never could: to strip away misuse, expose false authority, and return us to the God of love, grace, and accountability.

This is not a rejection of faith. It is a restoration of it.

May these pages help separate God from the harm done in His name and guide wounded hearts toward a faith that heals, a truth that frees, and a God who was never the author of their pain.

CONTENTS

Act IV

WHAT GOD WAS DOING THE WHOLE TIME

ABOUT THE AUTHOR

Carla Henry-Lewis writes for people who still believe there's something sacred out there—but aren't sure what to do with the version of faith they were handed.

She grew up fluent in Scripture, familiar with church culture, and well-acquainted with the disconnect between what people *say* they believe and how they actually live. Over time, that gap raised questions—about leadership, power, and who gets to speak for God—that couldn't be ignored or spiritualized away.

Rather than walk away from faith altogether, Carla chose a different path: curiosity over conformity, discernment over dogma, and fruit over noise.

Y'all Wanted a King is the first book in her **Spiritual Makeover Series**, which revisits familiar biblical stories without religious pressure or polished answers. The goal isn't to tell readers what to believe, but to invite them to look again—at Scripture, at leadership, and at the human tendency to hand our power over to the wrong voices.

Carla is also the creator of the **Stress Makeover™** framework and the author of several books on relationships, conflict, and emotional health. Her work blends insight, cultural awareness, and gentle humor, offering space for reflection rather than rules.

She writes for readers who are tired of spiritual performances, skeptical of easy answers, and still quietly hoping that truth—whatever it is—can survive honest questions.

If you're curious but cautious, questioning but open, you're welcome here.

INTRODUCTION

When Rebellion Looks Holy and Stubbornness Feels Like Strength

There is a scripture in the Bible that hit me like a slap the first time I read it with open eyes:

> *"For rebellion is as the sin of witchcraft, and stubbornness is as iniquity and idolatry."*

> — 1 SAMUEL 15:23

Witchcraft?

Idolatry?

Those were big, scary, *other people's* sins.

Not mine.

Never mine.

Surely not mine.

Like many Christians, I had my mental categories:

Witchcraft — absolutely not.

Idol worship — couldn't be me.

Rebellion and stubbornness — well... that's just my personality, right? A little feistiness. A little backbone. A little "I don't let people walk over me."

I saw witchcraft as a dark room filled with candles and pentagrams.

I saw idols as carved statues in ancient temples.

But rebellion?

Stubbornness?

Those were my "strengths."

At least, that's what I told myself.

Then Samuel's words cracked through my self-righteousness:

Rebellion is like witchcraft. Stubbornness is like idolatry.

Not similar.

Not "kind of like."

In God's eyes — equivalent.

It was as if God said:

"You think you're above those sins, but you are walking in them... you just renamed them so you could feel righteous."

And suddenly, I saw myself differently.

I saw the moments I dug my heels in, proud of my "discernment," when I was really resisting God.

I saw the moments I refused correction, thinking I was standing firm, when I was actually bowing at the altar of my own pride.

I saw the ways stubbornness became my idol, and rebellion my comfort, even as I judged everyone else's sins as more "serious" than mine.

That scripture humbled me.

It exposed me.

It rescued me.

And it opened my eyes to something deeper:

Pride and stubbornness go hand in hand. They just wear church clothes.

Which brings us to why this book exists.

A Nation That Chose Stubbornness Over Wisdom

In 1 Samuel, the people demanded a king.

Not because God told them to.

Not because it was righteous.

Not because it was wise.

But because everyone else had one — and they were determined to get what they wanted even when God warned them otherwise.

Israel thought their motives were pure. Their desires felt justified. They believed they were pursuing what was best for the nation.

But under the surface, their demand for a king was fueled by:

- insecurity
- pride
- rebellion
- stubbornness
- comparison
- fear
- and the desire to fit in with godless nations.

Samuel warned them.

They didn't listen.

(That stubbornness again.)

And God gave them what they asked for.

(Sometimes that's the worst kind of judgment.)

They didn't know the details.

They didn't know the timeline.

They didn't know David's name yet.

But they knew God would not abandon His people.

THE REMNANT STILL BELIEVES

When a nation forgets God, the remnant remembers Him.

Their prayers become a prophetic anchor.

"Lord, raise someone who sees You."

"Lord, raise someone who fears You more than people."

"Lord, raise someone who can heal what Saul broke."

"Lord, raise someone who will restore what was lost."

Their prayers didn't create David — but they made space for David.

The remnant doesn't produce the solution; **they prepare the ground for it.**

Even today, remnant believers scattered across communities, churches, families, and workplaces pray the world back into alignment even as the world rolls its eyes.

THE REMNANT SAW THE TRUTH EARLY

People addicted to a dysfunctional leader are always the last to notice the destruction.

But the remnant?

They see the writing on the wall.

They aren't fooled by:

- giftedness without maturity
- charisma without character
- confidence without wisdom
- strength without self-control
- passion without purpose

They pay attention to fruit while the nation drools over personality.

They warn long before the collapse.

Samuel warned.

The remnant listened.

The nation did not.

And that is why the remnant exists: **to hold truth steady until the nation is ready to hear it again.**

THE REMNANT STOOD BETWEEN COLLAPSE AND MERCY

If not for the remnant, Saul's collapse would have taken Israel down entirely.

But their prayers became the spiritual insulation that carried the nation through judgment into restoration. Their faithfulness attracted mercy even when the nation sowed foolishness.

They were the reason Israel survived long enough for God to raise David.

Quietly.

Faithfully.

Persistently.

The nation was not held together by political strategy or military strength — certainly not by Saul's emotional outbursts.

It was held together by people whose knees bent before God when everyone else bowed to fear and insecurity.

A Bridge to Restoration

Every nation goes through seasons of foolishness. Every generation wrestles with pride and idolatry. But restoration never begins with the majority.

It begins with the faithful few.

Israel didn't rise again because of programs, reforms, or politics.

They rose because a spiritually awake remnant held the door open long enough for God's mercy to rush in.

They stood between what was collapsing and what God was about to rebuild.

This is one of the holiest assignments in Scripture:

being the few who keep the light burning when the many have blown out their lamps.

Why This Book Exists

This book is not just satire.

It's not just political commentary.

It's not just biblical comparison.

It is a **love letter** to every nation, every community, every voter who has ever looked at the leadership they chose and asked:

"How did we get here?"

It is a reminder that:

- God has seen worse.
- He has survived worse.
- His people have survived worse.

And every foolish season eventually gives way to wisdom.

But first… we're going to talk about how y'all got here.

And Samuel will be right beside us, shaking his head, chuckling under his beard, saying:

"Child… this story is older than dirt."

PROLOGUE

SAMUEL STEPS INTO 2025

If you listen closely—really closely—you can almost hear the sound of sandals slapping against linoleum as an old prophet named Samuel strolls through a modern airport with a scroll tucked under his arm and a look on his face that says, *"I told y'all. I absolutely told y'all."*

He passes a Cinnabon, pauses, sniffs, and keeps walking. He's been resurrected into 2025 with one assignment: to witness what happens when a nation demands a king, ignores every warning, and then sits there blinking when the consequences show up like an overdue light bill.

Samuel has seen this movie before.

He saw it centuries ago when Israel went through the same identity crisis many nations face today: the season where being God's people somehow feels less appealing than being like everybody else. You see other nations with their big speeches, shiny crowns, and loud rulers commanding attention on the world stage. And something in you whispers:

"Why can't *we* have that?

Why can't we have someone strong?

Someone bold?

Someone loud enough to drown out all our insecurities?"

Samuel remembers that moment well. Israel's elders came to him—chests out, voices full of confidence but hearts full of insecurity—and said:

"Look, Sam... you're getting old. Your sons—bless their hearts—ain't it. Make us a king to judge us like all the other nations."

Ah yes. The most dangerous sentence in human history:

"Make us like everybody else."

That one sentence has launched wars, bankrupted families, broken marriages, fueled revolutions, and convinced people to buy things they absolutely did not need on late-night infomercials.

And now, as Samuel walks through this modern world—past Starbucks, past TVs blasting political commentary, past grown adults arguing on the internet—he recognizes the same spiritual disease he confronted in ancient Israel:

Discontentment mixed with insecurity, wrapped in the glittery paper of comparison.

Because that's always how it starts.

A nation doesn't wake up one morning and suddenly choose chaos.

It begins with a quiet envy:

"Well... look what *they* have."

It begins by craving the emotional comfort of a strongman, the thrill of a spectacle, the illusion of certainty during uncertain times.

And then, somewhere along the way, someone shouts:

"Give us a king!"

And the crowd claps like it's a praise break.

Samuel tried—Lord knows he tried—to warn his people. He spoke plainly, vividly, and in detail:

"He will take your sons.

He will take your daughters.

He will take your fields.

He will take your freedom.

He will take, take, take until you realize you've given him everything, and he's given you nothing but trouble."

But people don't like warnings.

Warnings interrupt fantasies.

And the consequences?

They arrive right on schedule.

A STORY THAT FEELS UNCOMFORTABLY FAMILIAR

This isn't just Israel's story.

It's ours.

We have lived—and *are living*—through a generation that chose its leaders based on insecurity, ego, nostalgia, outrage, and emotional cravings rather than wisdom, character, or discernment.

We didn't simply choose a Saul.

We demanded him.

And like Israel, we discovered a painful truth:

- Rebellion baptized in religious language is still rebellion.
- Stubbornness wrapped in patriotism is still idolatry.

- Pride justified as "discernment" is still pride.

We mistook stubbornness for strength and rebellion for boldness.

We mistook charisma for leadership and attention for authority.

And we learned—personally, nationally, spiritually—what Israel learned the hard way:

When you choose based on image, you will live with the consequences behind that image.

WHY THIS BOOK MATTERS NOW

Israel's story is not ancient history.

It is a **warning label**:

- For nations
- For churches
- For families
- For any of us who have ever chosen someone based on vibes
- For anyone who defended dysfunction out of tribal loyalty
- For anyone who dug their heels in because admitting the truth felt too humiliating

This book traces the cycle:

1. Wanting what everyone else has
2. Ignoring warnings
3. Choosing a Saul
4. Defending him out of pride
5. Suffering the fallout
6. Finally waking up

Israel wasn't stupid.

They were stubborn.

And I can't judge them too harshly, because I've been stubborn too. I've justified rebellion as personality. I've called pride "confidence." I've baptized stubbornness as "discernment." And I've learned—painfully—that when God calls something sin, I am not authorized to rename it.

This book is not written from a seat of judgment.

It is written from a seat of understanding.

From someone who has learned that obedience is freedom, humility is safety, and discernment only works when we admit we might be wrong.

MY PRAYER BEFORE YOU TURN THE PAGE

May this book humble us.

May it awaken us.

May it mature us.

May it save us from choosing another Saul because we refuse to admit we chose the last one for the wrong reasons.

May God give us the courage to examine ourselves before we examine our leaders.

Because leaders do not appear out of thin air— They rise from the desires of the people.

And if our desires are rooted in fear, pride, or stubbornness, we will always choose the wrong king.

May this be the generation that breaks the cycle.

Now… let's revisit the story.

ACT I

THE AUDACITY OF ASKING FOR WHAT YOU AREN'T READY FOR

1

WANNABE NATIONS: THE HUMAN OBSESSION WITH FITTING IN

WHEN IDENTITY ISN'T ENOUGH

H umans have many weaknesses—pride, fear, stubbornness, the inability to put the shopping cart back in the corral—but one weakness reigns above them all:

We hate being different.

We *say* we love uniqueness, but the truth?

Most people want to be distinct enough to be admired, but similar enough to blend in.

It's a delicate dance of ego and insecurity.

Israel mastered that dance first.

They were God's chosen people—handpicked, protected, fed in miraculous ways, guided by divine GPS systems like clouds and fire. They had direct access to the Creator of the universe, yet somehow still managed to look over the neighbor's fence and say:

"Heh... their system seems better than ours."

The Amalekites had a king.

The Moabites had a king.

The Philistines had a king with extra muscles and probably a generous military budget.

Other nations strutted around with rulers wearing crowns, waving scepters, and giving grand speeches.

And Israel—blessed, covered, chosen—looked at all that shine and said:

"Why can't we have one of those? Why we gotta be... special?"

Imagine being so blessed that you complain about being chosen.

Samuel tried to remind them:

"You literally have the living God as your ruler. You're good."

But Israel said, "Well, He's good, but He's not flashy. He doesn't hold rallies. He doesn't sit on thrones shouting decrees and waving golden spoons."

In modern terms, Israel didn't want the quiet, stable parent. They wanted the one who threw birthday parties with fireworks.

And here's where the satire writes itself:

They wanted what everyone else had—even if what everyone else had wasn't working for them either.

COMPARISON: THE FIRST CRACK IN THE FOUNDATION

Sound familiar?

Fast forward a few thousand years, and you'll find the same energy humming in modern political circles. A certain group—specifically those who once strode through history with cultural dominance—looked around and said:

"Uh oh... the world is changing. We're not the only voice in the room.

We don't like this feeling."

And instead of embracing maturity, shared power, or humility, some developed an Israel-level case of comparison fever.

They looked outward and whispered:

- "Maybe we need someone louder."
- "Maybe we need someone who will fight for us... whatever that means."
- "Maybe we need someone who reminds us of the good old days—even if those days weren't good for most people."

Just like Israel, they weren't looking for what worked.

They were looking for what *felt* comforting.

And comfort mixed with insecurity? Chile... that becomes a whole spiritual condition.

THE DESIRE TO BE LIKE "EVERYONE ELSE"

Israel didn't want a king because a king was necessary.

They wanted a king because everyone else had one.

Peer pressure is not a teenage problem.

It's a *human* problem.

Let's be honest: Israel had a chronic case of national FOMO.

They feared missing out on prestige.

They feared missing out on pageantry.

They feared missing out on being seen as legitimate on the world stage.

So instead of embracing their God-given identity—a chosen people led by the Creator—they mimicked nations that didn't even know which god to pray to on Tuesdays.

Modern voters caught the same bug.

As the country grew more diverse, more equitable, and more inclusive, they felt their old cultural dominance slipping. And nothing rattles an insecure heart like losing unspoken privilege.

Instead of adapting or growing, some looked at global strongmen and said:

"See? THAT is leadership!"

Israel looked to nations who oppressed them.

Modern voters looked to nations they claimed to fear.

But comparison doesn't have to make sense.

It only has to scratch the itch of insecurity.

WANNABE SYNDROME (A SPIRITUAL DIAGNOSIS)

Let's call this what it is:

Wannabe Syndrome.

It is the spiritual sickness that convinces healthy people to chase harmful things because those harmful things look shiny on someone else.

Wannabe Syndrome makes a perfectly good nation look at chaos and say, **"We want some."**

It makes a stable democracy drool over theatrical autocracy.

It makes people who have everything believe they have nothing unless they have what others do.

It convinces grown adults to follow leaders who talk like tantruming toddlers because "at least he's strong!"

It convinces people to trade boring stability for entertaining insta-bility—because they mistake drama for direction.

It convinced Israel to swap divine governance for Saul.

And it convinced modern voters to follow someone loud, defiant, unpredictable, and emotionally volatile—because he "looked strong."

Wannabe Syndrome produces one predictable fruit: **People forget who they are.**

Israel forgot they were God's people.

Modern voters forgot they were citizens, not subjects—a nation, not a fan club.

Insecure people always assume the grass is greener—never realizing the other nation's grass is fake turf glued down with propaganda.

THE CRAVING FOR A SYMBOL, NOT A LEADER

Israel didn't ask for a leader.

They asked for an image—a symbol—someone who *looked* powerful, regardless of the reality.

That same craving exists today.

Many modern voters weren't looking for character, policy, humility, or competence.

They were searching for a feeling.

A fantasy.

A king-like presence who could restore their sense of dominance.

Warnings never reached them because:

Warnings appeal to the mind.

Comparison seduces the heart.

And once insecurity seduces the heart, you could wave red flags the size of the Chrysler Building and they'll still shrug: "**Nobody's perfect.**"

Israel excused Saul early.

Modern voters excused their leader early.

Why?

Because comparison is emotional, not logical.

And fearful hearts don't want truth—they want reassurance.

WHEN NATIONS FORGET WHO THEY ARE

Comparison is always rooted in fear:

- Fear of losing power
- Fear of losing relevance
- Fear of losing identity
- Fear of no longer being special

That fear drove Israel straight into monarchy.

That fear drove modern voters straight into political chaos.

And both learned—too late—that:

- What *feels* powerful doesn't always lead to peace.
- What *looks* strong doesn't always lead to stability.
- What *sounds* bold doesn't always lead to wisdom.

The irony?

Israel wasn't meant to be like other nations.

They were meant to be set apart.

The modern conservative base—at its best—had an identity rooted in principle.

But fear cracked that identity.

Suddenly, they didn't want to be principled—they wanted to be powerful.

They didn't want to be different—they wanted to be dominant.

They didn't want to be steady—they wanted to be loud.

And so they did what Israel did: **They traded identity for imitation.**

How Nations Lose Themselves

Comparison is the gateway drug to foolishness.

Because once comparison takes root—

once insecurity takes over—

once people forget who they are—

They stop choosing leaders from purpose and start choosing them from panic.

And nothing good ever grows out of panic.

This is why this chapter matters.

Understanding how Israel got Saul is the only way to understand how modern America ended up choking on the fumes of a petulant king-like figure.

Not because people were evil.

Not because they were ignorant.

But because they were human—fragile, fearful, comparison-driven humans who wanted what everyone else had...

Even if it made no sense.

Even if it cost them everything.

Even if God Himself said,

"This is a terrible idea."

Whenever a nation trades identity for imitation, foolishness becomes inevitable.

And the only cure is remembering who you are—and who you were never meant to be.

2

THE AUDACITY OF IGNORING WARNINGS

THE ORIGINAL CVS-RECEIPT-LENGTH WARNING

H uman beings have a remarkable talent for ignoring warnings. It might be our most consistent spiritual gift.

We ignore warning labels on hair products, microwavable burritos, medicine bottles, and relationships we should've left in Season 1. The phrase "**Do not attempt**" has never stopped a single person who believed they were the exception.

Warnings, we assume, are for *other* people.

Other families.

Other nations.

Other voters.

Israel perfected this mindset first.

SAMUEL DIDN'T WHISPER THE TRUTH — HE MEGAPHONED IT

When Israel demanded a king, Samuel didn't hint. He didn't imply.

He didn't clear his throat and hope they caught on.

Samuel pulled out the prophetic megaphone and announced a list longer than a CVS receipt:

"He will take your sons.

He will take your daughters.

He will take your vineyards.

He will take your freedom.

He will take your sanity.

He will take your peace.

He will take everything—and then ask you to say 'thank you.'"

Samuel essentially said:

"This man is going to take and take and take..."

And Israel blinked, smiled politely, and replied: **"Right, right... but does he have charisma though?"**

They heard the words.

But their hearts whispered:

"We can handle it."

Translation?

"We think we're smarter than consequences."

WHY WARNINGS DON'T WORK ON DETERMINED PEOPLE

Children touch hot stoves for that reason.

Adults choose hot messes for that reason.

Nations elect hot tempers for that reason.

Israel believed they were the exception to God's wisdom.

Modern voters?

Not much different.

Before they hitched their wagon to a certain leader, experts were practically standing on rooftops shouting:

- "This won't end well."
- "This is unstable energy."
- "This is volatile behavior."
- "This isn't leadership — it's theatrics with emotional sparkles."

But the people waved them off like gnats at a picnic.

- "Shhh... he talks strong."
- "Shhh... he says what we want to say."
- "Shhh... he makes our enemies mad."
- "Shhh... he's not politically correct."

Translation?

"We like the show. Leave us alone."

There is a very particular kind of arrogance—ancient, holy, bold—that convinces people that the warnings that applied to every civilization in history will somehow skip them.

THE PSYCHOLOGY BEHIND IGNORING WARNINGS

Ignoring warnings isn't just foolishness.

It's *identity protection.*

If the king is wrong,

then maybe they made a bad decision.

If the king is unstable,

then maybe they ignored the warning signs.

If the king is unfit,

then maybe they were seduced by charisma and fear.

And people will burn down an entire country before they admit they misjudged someone.

Israel wasn't protecting Saul.

They were protecting their pride.

Modern voters weren't protecting their leader.

They were protecting their self-image.

DOUBLING DOWN: THE ANCIENT SPIRITUAL OLYMPICS

Once people emotionally invest in a leader, logic becomes optional.

Discernment becomes blurry.

Admitting fault becomes a spiritual CrossFit workout no one signed up for.

You could stack evidence to the ceiling.

You could hold up red flags the size of Manhattan.

You could show them receipts, video clips, transcripts, scandals, and meltdowns.

Still, they would say:

"He's being strong."

"He's just honest."

"They pushed him."

"He's draining the swamp."

"He's playing chess while everyone else plays checkers."

The mental gymnastics could've qualified for the Olympics.

This is exactly what Samuel saw in Saul's hype squad:

- Saul was jealous? "David needs to stay humble."
- Saul threw spears? "He's under stress."
- Saul disobeyed God? "Well… he didn't mean it like that."

There was always a spin.

Always a justification.

Always a fresh coat of denial paint.

Because once a leader becomes your identity, admitting he's flawed feels like admitting *you* are.

WHY WARNINGS HIT THE MIND, BUT COMPARISON HITS THE HEART

This is the deeper truth:

Warnings appeal to the mind.

Comparison seduces the heart.

Israel wasn't craving leadership.

They were craving validation.

Modern voters weren't craving policy.

They were craving representation—someone who made them feel seen in a changing world.

When people are desperate to feel seen, they will follow anyone who promises:

"I alone can fix it."

Fear of losing power.

Fear of losing relevance.

Fear of losing identity.

Fear of not being special anymore.

That fear drove Israel into monarchic disaster.

That fear drove modern voters into political chaos.

And both groups learned too late:

- What feels powerful doesn't always lead to peace.
- What looks strong doesn't always lead to stability.
- What sounds bold doesn't always lead to wisdom.

WHEN GOD LETS CONSEQUENCES TEACH

Here is the part no one likes:

Sometimes God lets us have what we demanded—not because it's good—but because consequences are the only teacher we'll listen to.

Samuel wasn't being dramatic. He was being merciful.

He knew what they didn't want to admit:

A king chosen from insecurity will always rule from insecurity.

A nation ruled by insecurity will always descend into fear.

A people guided by fear will always ignore truth.

But here's the hope Samuel held then, and the hope we hold now:

Even when people choose wrong, the story doesn't end there. God always positions a better leader.

A remnant always rises.

Wisdom eventually wins.

And consequences—though painful—have a way of clearing the fog.

This Chapter Matters because understanding Israel's refusal to heed Samuel's warnings is the key to understanding our own era.

Israel wasn't foolish because they ignored God.

They were foolish because they believed they could outsmart consequences.

Modern voters weren't foolish because they followed a man.

They were foolish because they trusted their feelings more than their discernment.

Both needed wisdom.

Both rejected it.

Both paid for it.

But both discovered—eventually—that God still writes redemption into human stubbornness.

This chapter reminds us:

When we ignore warnings, we don't escape consequences. We enroll in them.

And God, in His mercy, knows how to use even our worst choices to lead us back to truth.

3

THE CROWN THEY THOUGHT
WOULD SAVE THEM

CHOOSING STYLE OVER SUBSTANCE

E very generation eventually learns the same painful truth:
**If you choose a leader based on appearance, you will live
with the consequences behind that appearance.**

Israel learned this the hard way.

They wanted a king who *looked* the part.

Someone imposing. Someone impressive.

Someone tall enough to distract them from their insecurities.

And God — who never forces wisdom on the unwilling — let them
have exactly what they asked for.

Not a warrior.

Not a strategist.

Not a man of character.

Not a leader shaped by obedience.

Just... tall.

Tall enough to stand out in a crowd.

Tall enough to make them feel like they finally "arrived."

Tall enough to convince anxious people their fears were unfounded.

Saul's height became their security blanket.

And when a nation mistakes a security blanket for a leader, disaster is already stretching in the doorway.

THE CROWN THEY CHOSE FOR THEMSELVES

Saul didn't rise because he was righteous. He rose because he was aesthetically pleasing.

Scripture says it plainly:

He stood head and shoulders above everyone else.

Israel took one look and said:

"Yes. That one."

Height became holiness.

Swagger became strength.

Appearance became authority.

They didn't ask:

- Does he listen to God?
- Does he have discipline?
- Does he have integrity?
- Does he know how to lead?
- Does he understand responsibility?

No.

The national selection committee boiled it down to:

"Does he look like he could win a debate simply by standing up straight?"

In modern terms:

They hired a handsome influencer for a job that required a whole soul.

WHY PEOPLE FALL FOR STYLE OVER SUBSTANCE

This isn't ancient foolishness.

This is human foolishness.

People still choose leaders the same way:

- Loudness mistaken for strength
- Confidence mistaken for competence
- Charisma mistaken for character
- Image mistaken for substance
- Branding mistaken for wisdom

And here's the spiritual danger:

When people choose from insecurity, they choose someone who reflects their insecurity — not someone who heals it.

Saul didn't fix Israel's identity crisis.

He magnified it.

This is why insecure nations gravitate toward insecure leaders: they see themselves in him and call it strength.

A nation cannot outsource its internal brokenness onto a leader and expect wholeness in return.

THE ILLUSION OF STRENGTH

Saul *looked* strong.

He projected power.

He carried himself like a man who believed his own press releases.

But the text reveals the truth:

He had no internal foundation.

He was emotionally flammable.

Easily threatened.

Deeply insecure.

Driven by fear instead of conviction.

Shaken by other people's praise.

Obsessed with image management.

Saul was tall, yes.

But he was cracked on the inside.

And insecure leaders always damage the people they lead — because they cannot handle anything that exposes their own emptiness.

Israel didn't see that at first. Nobody sees cracks in the crown until the glitter chips off.

WHEN HEIGHT BECOMES A LEADERSHIP STRATEGY

Saul's résumé could have fit on a Post-it:

Tall. Handsome. Presentable.

Imagine basing the destiny of a nation on a man who could model for a billboard but couldn't manage his own fears.

But Israel was intoxicated with optics.

They didn't want depth.

They wanted display.

They didn't want spiritual maturity.

They wanted social proof.

They didn't want obedience.

They wanted aesthetics.

And here's the twist:

God warned them.

Samuel warned them.

History warned them.

Common sense tried to wave a flag.

But comparison drowned out discernment.

This is what happens when insecurity drives the selection process: **People pick what looks good, not what *is* good.**

THE MODERN PARALLELS NOBODY WANTS TO ADMIT

We've seen this show in modern times too.

Crowds swooning over leaders who:

- look confident
- sound bold
- deliver theatrics
- provoke enemies
- project toughness
- master performance

People confuse entertainment with leadership.

Crowd control with wisdom.

Defiance with courage.

Ego with strength.

And when the real person behind the performance emerges, the nation is already emotionally invested in the illusion.

Saul's story is more than biblical.

It is psychological.

Cultural.

Political.

Human.

People crave the illusion of strength when they feel internally weak.

Which is why style-based decisions never end well.

WHEN SUBSTANCE ARRIVES, THE CONTRAST IS PAINFUL

The tragedy of Saul wasn't just that he lacked substance.

The tragedy was that Israel no longer recognized substance when it appeared.

After choosing style, everything real feels underwhelming:

- Real humility feels too quiet.
- Real discipline feels too boring.
- Real leadership feels too steady.
- Real wisdom feels too slow.
- Real character feels too ordinary.

Saul conditioned them to think leadership was spectacle.

So when David showed up — calm, faithful, grounded — they didn't know what to do with a leader who wasn't performing.

This is why nations stay addicted to unhealthy leaders:

Once you get used to chaos, peace feels suspicious.

Once you get used to noise, truth feels too quiet.

Once you get used to style, substance feels disappointing.

But sometimes disappointment is the doorway to discernment.

THE LESSON ISRAEL NEEDED — AND WE STILL NEED

Saul is the biblical embodiment of what happens when a nation chooses:

- image over integrity
- charisma over character
- height over holiness
- style over substance
- performance over purpose

He was everything they wanted

and nothing they needed.

This is the danger of choosing from insecurity:

A wounded heart will always choose someone who matches the wound — not the healing.

Israel didn't need a tall king.

They needed a stable one.

They didn't need a celebrity.

They needed a shepherd.

But until people recognize the emptiness in their own desires,

they will choose crowns that glitter more than they guide.

Saul teaches us this:

If you choose a leader because he looks the part, you will eventually discover he cannot play the part.

And the cost of that discovery is always higher than the price of patience.

4

THE PETULANT KING HANDBOOK

WHEN A NATION MISTAKES
IMMATURITY FOR LEADERSHIP

S ome leaders rise because of wisdom.

Some rise because of character.

And some rise because the people's discernment took a sabbatical.

Saul falls squarely into the third category.

The man behaved less like a king and more like someone who needed a juice box, a nap, and a designated adult. He ruled Israel with the emotional stability of a wet firecracker — loud, unpredictable, and guaranteed to leave somebody burned.

Israel didn't just get a king.

They got **the Petulant King Starter Pack**.

And once he took the throne, it became clear: **If maturity were currency, Saul would've been bankrupt.**

LESSON 1: MAKE EVERY DECISION A MOOD SWING

Good leaders regulate emotions.

Petulant kings weaponize them.

Saul governed like his feelings were national policy. If he was happy, the nation sighed in relief. If he was irritated, the whole palace trembled. If someone praised David? Well... time to throw spears again.

His leadership philosophy could be summarized as:

"If I feel it, it must be true."

Saul's moods didn't just shift — they ricocheted.

One moment he was prophesying.

The next moment he was plotting.

One moment he was hugging David.

The next he was aiming a spear at the boy's head.

Imagine living under a king whose emotional state determined the national weather forecast.

"Today's outlook: sunny with a 60% chance of royal meltdown."

Israel learned quickly:

You don't follow a petulant king.

You survive him.

LESSON 2: BLAME EVERYONE ELSE — ALWAYS

Petulant kings are allergic to responsibility.

Every bad decision had an accomplice:

- The people made him do it.
- The enemy provoked him.
- Samuel took too long.
- David shined too brightly.
- The soldiers pressured him.
- The circumstances were unreasonable.

Saul had an entire encyclopedia of excuses and never once flipped to the "accountability" section.

He mastered the art of looking guilty while insisting he was innocent.

He could deliver a full apology with zero actual repentance.

You know the type:

"I'm sorry you feel that way."

Not: **"I'm sorry I did that."**

Modern readers recognize this pattern instantly — because we've watched leaders today spin their failures with the same energy as Saul, surrounded by hype squads who translate his chaos into "strategic genius."

LESSON 3: TURN LEADERSHIP INTO A PERSONAL THERAPY SESSION

Instead of confronting his insecurity, Saul used national power to soothe it.

Every challenge threatened him.

Every gifted person intimidated him.

Every successful soldier made him paranoid.

David's victories?

Triggers.

The people's songs?

Triggers.

Anyone with confidence?

Triggers.

Saul didn't need a crown;

he needed counseling.

But insecure leaders don't pursue healing.

They pursue control.

They punish people who remind them of their inadequacy.

They chase validation like oxygen.

They build systems around themselves instead of building nations.

Under Saul, Israel was not being governed.

They were being emotionally managed.

LESSON 4: CONFUSE NOISE FOR STRENGTH

Saul talked big.

Acted big.

Projected big.

But projection is not power.

And noise is not leadership.

He created drama to feel relevant.

He stirred conflict to feel powerful.

He made impulsive declarations to feel decisive.

Israel mistook all that noise for strength — until the day came when they needed stability, wisdom, and clarity, and discovered their king had none of the above.

It is a tragic moment in any nation when the people realize:

"Oh... we chose a performer, not a leader."

LESSON 5: SURROUND YOURSELF WITH ENABLERS

Petulant kings cannot survive without an entourage willing to clap for foolishness.

Saul had one.

They didn't protect the nation.

They protected Saul's ego.

They affirmed his worst impulses.

They justified his spirals.

They spun his rants.

They apologized for his tantrums.

They reframed his insecurity as "passion."

To stay in favor, they became interpreters of nonsense.

Sound familiar?

Modern hype squads do the same — just with microphones, social media accounts, matching T-shirts, podcast studios, and a full merch line.

The packaging has changed.

The psychology hasn't.

LESSON 6: USE POWER TO PUNISH RATHER THAN PROTECT

Leadership exists for the good of the people.

Petulant kings use leadership for the preservation of self.

When Saul felt threatened, he lashed out — not at enemies, but at those assigned to help him.

His jealousy nearly killed Jonathan.

His insecurity drove David into exile.

His fear destabilized the military.

His paranoia drained the nation's morale.

And worst of all:

Israel became collateral damage in Saul's emotional battles.

A king's inner life always becomes a nation's outer experience.

This is why Scripture and history are united on one truth:

Insecure leaders fracture everything they touch.

LESSON 7: SPIRITUALIZE DISOBEDIENCE

The most dangerous petulant king behavior is not the tantrum.

It is the tendency to baptize disobedience in religious language.

Saul said all the right phrases:

"I did obey the Lord."

"The people pressured me."

"I spared these animals for worship."

"I was acting for God's glory."

But obedience is not measured by how holy you sound — it's measured by whether you did what God said.

Saul cloaked rebellion in worship vocabulary.

He weaponized spirituality to justify sin.

Modern leaders do the same when they wrap chaos in patriotism, cruelty in righteousness, or pride in prayer language.

The vocabulary is familiar.

The spirit behind it is not.

THE DEEP TRAGEDY OF THE PETULANT KING

Saul did not ruin Israel because he was evil.

He ruined Israel because he was **immature**.

And maturity is the foundation of every righteous leader.

Without it:

- Power becomes toxic
- Decisions become impulsive
- Relationships become transactional
- Criticism becomes threat
- Correction becomes offense
- Humility becomes impossible

Saul's downfall was not a sudden collapse.

It was the slow unraveling of a man who never grew up.

And when a leader refuses maturity, the nation suffers the consequences.

Israel asked for a king who looked powerful.

God let them see what happens when "powerful-looking" is all you choose.

Saul teaches us:

- Talent without discipline is dangerous
- Charisma without character is chaotic
- Position without emotional maturity is destructive
- Insecurity masquerading as strength corrodes everything
- Leaders who refuse correction become leaders who create crisis

Petulant kings don't just fall.

They take people with them.

And God, in His mercy, uses their collapse to teach generations what to never choose again.

This chapter prepares the ground for the contrast that's coming:

After witnessing Saul, the nation is finally ready to appreciate David — not because David is flashy, but because he is faithful.

5

WHEN LEADERSHIP IS AN EPISODE OF JERRY SPRINGER

CHAOS-DRIVEN GOVERNANCE AND A NATION THAT FORGOT IT DESERVED BETTER

S ome leaders govern nations.

Some govern crises.

And some govern like guests on an old episode of *Jerry Springer* — all drama, no dignity, and a crowd wondering how they got seats to this show.

Under Saul, leadership became a spectacle of emotional outbursts, rash decisions, paranoid accusations, and public meltdowns. Israel found itself living inside a reality show long before reality shows existed.

Every day felt like a new episode:

"Today on *The Royal Springer Show*:

A king who throws spears, a prophet who's exhausted, a faithful soldier on the run, and a nation held hostage by one man's insecurity!"

But the worst part?

Israel kept watching.

They normalized the chaos because they didn't know what healthy leadership felt like anymore.

CHAOS WASN'T THE SYMPTOM — IT WAS THE STRATEGY

Bad leaders don't accidentally create chaos.

They rely on it.

Chaos becomes camouflage for incompetence.

It keeps people distracted.

It keeps critics off-balance.

It keeps followers emotionally invested in the drama instead of holding the leader accountable.

Saul's reign was not one long mistake — it was a cycle:

1. **Emotional outburst**
2. **Rash decision**
3. **Momentary regret**
4. **Blame-shifting**
5. **A new crisis to replace the old one**

Sound familiar?

Modern times have shown us the same pattern:

A leader creates chaos, then declares himself the only one who can fix the chaos he created — and somehow, people fall for it.

Chaos becomes a leadership economy.

Drama becomes a currency.

Stability becomes the enemy.

Prophets Watching From the Sidelines Like: "This Is Y'all King?"

Samuel had front-row seats to the dysfunction.

Imagine being a prophet with a divine assignment, watching your nation's leader:

- Throw weapons in meetings
- Declare impulsive bans nobody asked for
- Break his own rules
- Consult shady advisors
- Make military decisions based on mood swings
- Ruin alliances
- Sabotage victories
- Spiral into paranoia mid-sentence

There is a specific kind of exhaustion reserved for those who must watch a leader self-destruct in slow motion.

Samuel wasn't judgmental — he was tired.

He had warned them.

He had pleaded with them.

He had prayed for them.

But when people insist on choosing a bad king, prophets become spectators at a national trainwreck.

Why the People Stayed in the Dysfunction

People don't cling to chaos because it's enjoyable. They cling because chaos becomes familiar.

Israel adapted:

- They walked on eggshells.
- They tiptoed around the king's moods.
- They pretended his meltdowns were "passion."
- They excused his emotional instability as "strong leadership."
- They explained away the spirals as "stress."

When foolishness is repeated long enough, it starts to sound like normalcy.

And when people have tied their identity to a leader, they will defend him even when his behavior is indefensible.

Israel didn't just follow Saul.

They became emotionally entangled with him.

That's why they didn't leave the show.

That's why they kept watching the episodes.

They had forgotten what peace felt like.

A NATION HELD HOSTAGE BY ONE MAN'S INNER BATTLES

Saul's internal turmoil spilled across the land.

His fear became national fear.

His panic became national panic.

His instability became national instability.

The entire nation lived inside his emotional climate.

When he spiraled, the nation trembled.

When he obsessed over David, the military stalled.

When he made impulsive vows, soldiers starved.

When he raged, families suffered.

When he crumbled, morale sank.

Israel wasn't simply enduring a bad leader.

They were absorbing his psychological collapse.

And this is the brutal truth:

A nation always absorbs the emotional health of its leader — for better or for worse.

WHEN GOVERNANCE BECOMES ENTERTAINMENT

One of the darkest signs of decline is when leadership stops being respected and starts being consumed like content.

Saul's erratic decisions created:

- spectacle
- scandal
- gossip
- confusion
- drama
- polarization
- fear
- shock value

He governed like he needed ratings.

And Israel, worn down from years of unpredictability, reacted the way exhausted people react everywhere:

They stopped demanding wisdom

and started craving distraction.

When a nation grows accustomed to chaos, it becomes emotionally numb.

And numb people tolerate what wise people would never allow.

THE COST OF A CHAOTIC LEADER

The fallout of Saul's emotionally unstable governance was not limited to the palace.

The ripple effects seeped into:

- **families** — divided by loyalty
- **friendships** — strained under tension
- **the military** — weakened by inconsistency
- **the priesthood** — burdened by crisis
- **the community** — operating in fear
- **the economy** — shaking under instability
- **the nation** — spiritually disoriented

Chaos always costs more than people expect.

And the bill always comes due.

Every Episode Revealed the Same Truth: Saul Was Unwell

This chapter of Israel's history reads like a case study in leadership psychology.

Saul was not wicked by nature.

He was unraveling emotionally.

He was spiritually fractured.

He was insecure, reactive, suspicious, exhausted, and overwhelmed.

And instead of seeking healing, he reached for control.

Instead of humbling himself, he clung to the throne.

Instead of admitting weakness, he performed strength.

He didn't need the crown.

He needed deliverance.

But a petulant king rarely steps down willingly.

Chaos is not entertainment.

Chaos is a warning.

Israel didn't realize how unhealthy Saul was until the consequences hit every part of national life.

But here is the mercy hidden in the madness:

Chaos prepares people to desire stability.

Foolishness prepares people to value wisdom.

Saul prepares people to recognize David.

Sometimes God lets a nation experience the full weight of a leader's immaturity

so they will never again confuse instability with strength.

Saul's chaos taught Israel what character actually looks like.

And it set the stage for a leader whose strength would not come from volume, intimidation, or spectacle — but from integrity, humility, and obedience.

ACT II

THE COLLAPSE OF WHAT THEY CHOSE

6

THE FOLLOWERS WHO ENABLED THE FOOLISHNESS

WHY PEOPLE DEFEND DYSFUNCTION — ANCIENT AND MODERN

A king like Saul cannot destroy a nation alone. He needs followers who will:

- defend him,
- excuse him,
- reinterpret his failures,
- rewrite his motives,
- and turn his insecurities into national identity.

Israel had an entire hype squad committed to protecting Saul's ego — not because he was wise, but because he made *them* feel important. Their proximity to his power felt like power.

And when Saul spun into jealousy, paranoia, poor decisions, and tear-streaked tantrums?

They stood beside the throne like human-sized affirmation stickers:

"That wasn't a tantrum — he was expressing passion."

"He didn't overreact — he just cares deeply."

"He's not unstable — people keep pushing his buttons."

Sound familiar?

Modern politics has perfected the same routine — just with microphones, hashtags, podcasts, and matching T-shirts.

The packaging changed.

The psychology didn't.

WHY PEOPLE DEFEND DYSFUNCTION

People don't defend bad leaders because the leader is strong.

They defend bad leaders because *they* need to feel strong.

A leader becomes a mirror.

If the king is wrong, then maybe *they* made a bad decision.

If the king is unstable, then maybe *they* ignored the warning signs.

If the king is morally compromised, then maybe *their* judgment wasn't as sound as they believed.

To avoid facing that truth, they build elaborate justification systems:

- "He's just honest."
- "He's saying what we all think."
- "He's fighting for us."
- "He's playing chess while everyone else plays checkers."

The mental gymnastics could qualify for Olympic medals.

This isn't stupidity — it's *identity protection*.

Once people tether their sense of self to a leader, any criticism of that leader feels like an attack on them personally. They defend him to defend themselves.

THE PSYCHOLOGY OF DOUBLING DOWN

Have you ever watched someone realize they made a terrible choice but still fight tooth and nail to prove they were right?

That's doubling down.

Israel's hype squad was the blueprint:

- Saul gets jealous of David? **"David needs to stay humble."**
- Saul throws spears? **"He's under pressure."**
- Saul disobeys God explicitly? **"He didn't mean it that way."**
- Saul makes irrational decrees? **"He's just decisive."**

It didn't matter how glaring the red flags were.

They would sand them down, repaint them gold, and call them "unique leadership qualities."

Modern hype squads follow the same script:

- Wild comments? "He tells it like it is."
- Lies? "He's speaking his truth."
- Meltdowns? "He has passion."
- Scandals? "It's a witch hunt."

Once people commit emotionally, facts become negotiable.

Reality becomes elastic.

Discernment becomes optional.

WHY ADMITTING THEY WERE WRONG FEELS IMPOSSIBLE

To acknowledge a leader's dysfunction means confronting the uncomfortable truth:

"I misjudged someone."

Nobody likes that feeling.

So instead of repenting, people reinforce their loyalty:

- They look for information that confirms their choice.
- They avoid anything that challenges their choice.
- They reinterpret criticism as persecution.
- They elevate loyalty above integrity.

This is why both ancient and modern hype squads grow more extreme over time.

They are not defending the king —

they are defending their *identity*,

their *pride*,

their *previous votes*,

their *public declarations*,

their *community belonging*.

Loyalty becomes a shield for shame.

THE COST OF ENABLING A PETULANT KING

Enablers aren't harmless bystanders.

They are active participants in the unraveling.

Israel's enablers:

- Encouraged Saul to chase David
- Reinforced his insecurity
- Nurtured his paranoia
- Protected his ego

- Rewarded his emotional instability
- Helped create the environment where disobedience flourished

Modern enablers do the same when they:

- Promote misinformation
- Spin chaos into heroism
- Attack truth-tellers
- Punish dissent
- Redefine loyalty as righteousness
- Mock accountability as weakness

Enablers build altars to bad leadership.

And once the altar is built, tearing it down feels like tearing down part of themselves.

THE SPIRITUAL TRAP: LOYALTY AS RIGHTEOUSNESS

Saul's followers believed loyalty was godliness.

"Stand with the king.

Protect the king.

Defend the king at all costs."

But here's the irony:

Their loyalty to Saul became disloyalty to God.

This is what happens when a leader becomes an idol.

Loyalty becomes distorted.

Faith becomes politicized.

Truth becomes negotiable.

Morality becomes situational.

Obedience becomes optional.

People think they are honoring leadership,

but they are actually enabling dysfunction.

And God — who sees clearly — is not impressed.

WHEN ENABLERS ATTACK THE TRUTH-TELLERS

Both ancient Israel and modern societies follow this pattern:

The more unstable the leader becomes, the more hostile the followers grow toward anyone who tells the truth.

Samuel warned Saul — and they resented him.

David behaved honorably — and they targeted him.

Wise voices spoke up — and were pushed aside.

Truth becomes threat when a lie has become identity.

The prophet is labeled "divisive."

The truth-teller is labeled "disloyal."

The critic is labeled "enemy."

This is not politics.

This is spiritual dysfunction.

Enablers must silence truth to protect their illusion.

IN THE END, ENABLERS AREN'T PROTECTING THE KING — THEY'RE PROTECTING THEMSELVES

Israel's defenders of Saul eventually faced a painful truth:

Their loyalty didn't save the king.

It only prolonged the national suffering.

Modern enablers will discover the same reality.

Because here is the constant:

A leader who refuses accountability will always collapse — and the people who propped him up will absorb the fallout.

The tragedy of Saul's enablers is not that they defended a broken man.

It's that they confused loyalty with righteousness, fear with faithfulness, and noise with wisdom.

Leaders do not fall in isolation.

They are carried by the hands of those who excused their impulses, defended their tantrums,

and baptized their disobedience in spiritual language.

This chapter teaches us:

- Followers shape leaders as much as leaders shape followers.
- Loyalty to dysfunction is not faithfulness — it is bondage.
- Defending a leader is not the same as discerning a leader.
- You cannot cling to a Saul and walk in wisdom at the same time.

And most importantly:

A nation can survive a bad leader faster than it can survive the people who insist he is good.

7

PROPHETS, TRUTH-TELLERS & OTHER PEOPLE NOBODY LIKES

WHY ACCOUNTABILITY FEELS OFFENSIVE — UNTIL THE COLLAPSE

E very generation has two kinds of leaders:

1. The ones people *want* to hear
2. The ones people *need* to hear

Samuel belonged to the second category — and that alone guaranteed he would never win a popularity contest.

Prophets aren't entertainers.

They aren't hype men.

They don't exist to soothe feelings or affirm delusion.

They exist to tell the truth when the truth is deeply inconvenient.

Which is exactly why nobody likes them.

People prefer kings who flatter their insecurities over prophets who expose them.

TRUTH-TELLERS ARE ALWAYS MISUNDERSTOOD BEFORE THE COLLAPSE

Before everything falls apart, truth-tellers sound "negative."

After everything falls apart, truth-tellers sound "wise."

Nothing about the truth changed — only the people did.

Samuel warned Israel:

- about their motives
- about their insecurity
- about Saul's limitations
- about the consequences
- about their stubbornness

But people who are determined to get their way will always interpret caution as criticism.

Truth becomes annoying.

Warnings become noise.

Discernment becomes "judgmental."

Accountability becomes "disrespect."

People don't want prophets when they're chasing a fantasy.

They want prophets when the fantasy crashes.

And by then, the damage is already done.

THE ANATOMY OF REJECTING A PROPHET

When people don't want to hear the truth, they follow a predictable spiritual pattern:

1. **Dismiss the messenger**
   - "He's too harsh."
   - "He's outdated."
   - "He doesn't understand."
2. **Redefine the message**
   - "It wasn't that bad."
   - "He's exaggerating."
3. **Normalize the sin**
   - "Everybody does it."
   - "It's not that serious."
4. **Attack the motive**
   - "He just doesn't like our king."
   - "He's biased."
5. **Wait until consequences hit**
   - Then suddenly:
     - "Where is Samuel? Somebody call him, please!"
     - This is why prophets always seem grieved, tired, or introverted.
     - They see the iceberg long before the ship feels the impact.

SAUL'S FRAGILE EGO COULDN'T HANDLE TRUTH

For truth to work, the listener must have humility.

Saul had none.

Every time Samuel confronted him:

- Saul deflected
- Saul minimized
- Saul spiritualized
- Saul blamed others
- Saul convinced himself he was still right

Samuel tried to correct him.

Saul tried to correct the narrative.

This is the hallmark of insecure leaders:

They don't repent — they rebrand.

Saul didn't want truth.

He wanted validation.

He didn't want correction.

He wanted applause.

Truth destabilizes insecure people because validation—not right-eousness—is their real god.

WHY TRUTH-TELLERS GET EXILED

People exiled Samuel emotionally long before they stopped listening physically.

Because accountability is uncomfortable.

Correction is painful.

Clarity is confrontational.

And prophets bring all three.

Truth-tellers threaten idols.

Truth-tellers expose motives.

Truth-tellers interrupt fantasies.

Truth-tellers prevent people from worshiping a leader.

So when a king becomes a god in people's hearts, prophets become the enemy.

That's why Samuel was marginalized, dismissed, ignored, and treated like the grumpy uncle who always ruins the party with perspective.

Modern truth-tellers experience the same:

- journalists silenced
- pastors sidelined
- teachers attacked
- whistleblowers discredited
- counselors dismissed
- voices of reason mocked

Truth is rarely welcomed during seasons of national delusion.

WHEN THE NATION FINALLY WOKE UP

There comes a moment in every era of foolishness when people look around and whisper:

"Something is very wrong here."

The veneer cracks.

The fantasy dims.

The consequences arrive.

The crisis intensifies.

The dysfunction becomes undeniable.

And suddenly — the truth that was offensive becomes the truth that is needed.

Samuel didn't change.

The nation did.

Because consequences create clarity.

When Saul spiraled beyond denial,

when the damage became visible,

when the cost could no longer be hidden.

Israel didn't ask for more spectacle.

They asked for wisdom.

Prophets always outlast kings.

Not because they want to.

But because truth does.

TRUTH-TELLING IS A SPIRITUAL ASSIGNMENT, NOT A PERSONALITY TYPE

People often imagine prophets as angry, dramatic personalities.

But biblical truth-tellers were usually:

- gentle
- reluctant
- grieved
- burdened
- emotionally exhausted

They didn't speak because they enjoyed it.

They spoke because God required it.

Truth-telling is obedience, not performance.

Some truth-tellers today are pastors.

Some are teachers.

Some are coworkers.

Some are family members.

Some are friends who quietly whisper, "This isn't healthy."

Their courage keeps communities from collapsing.

Prophets are not glamorous.

They're necessary.

When a nation honors kings but silences prophets, destruction is guaranteed.

Truth-tellers are God's early warning system.

They are the brakes before the cliff.

The lighthouse before the storm.

The clarity before the consequences.

But people must choose to listen.

This chapter reminds us:

- Truth feels uncomfortable before it feels helpful
- Correction feels offensive before it feels protective
- Prophets are resented before they are respected
- Accountability is rejected before it is recognized as mercy

And the most painful reality:

People don't dislike prophets because of the truth they speak.

People dislike prophets because the truth they speak exposes the lies they trust.

Prophets aren't sent to win popularity.

They're sent to keep the nation alive long enough for God to raise someone better.

WHEN A NATION STARTS TO COME APART AT THE SEAMS

THE SLOW, PAINFUL UNRAVELING UNDER A DYSFUNCTIONAL KING

N ations rarely collapse overnight.

They erode.

Slowly.

Quietly.

Invisibly at first.

People imagine collapse as a dramatic boom — a sudden moment when everything catches fire. But the truth is more unsettling:

Collapse begins with tiny compromises, normalized dysfunction, and loyalty that blinds people to reality.

Under Saul, Israel didn't fall because the Philistines were too strong.

Israel fell because Saul was too unstable — and the people were too invested in him to admit it.

A nation cannot stay whole when its leader is coming apart.

IT DIDN'T START WITH WAR — IT STARTED WITH WEARINESS

By the time Saul's failures became obvious, the people were already spiritually exhausted.

They weren't cheering anymore.

They weren't inspired anymore.

They weren't confident anymore.

They were tired.

Tired of chaos.

Tired of unpredictable decrees.

Tired of emotional instability.

Tired of being jerked between paranoia and pride.

Tired of watching the throne shake while pretending everything was fine.

A weary nation becomes a divided nation — because exhaustion always reveals what denial hides.

DIVISION WAS NOT LOUD AT FIRST — IT WAS SUBTLE

Division rarely starts with shouting.

It starts with silence.

Israel began whispering in small pockets:

- "Something feels off."
- "This isn't how a king should act."
- "Are we sure we're on the right path?"
- "Didn't Samuel warn us about this?"

When truth breaks through, people experience it privately long before they admit it publicly.

Meanwhile, Saul's loyalists doubled down harder than ever.

The more obvious the dysfunction became, the more fiercely they defended him.

That's how division grows:

Not from honest disagreement, but from competing versions of reality.

The remnant saw truth.

The enablers saw a threat.

And in the middle stood a nation that no longer knew what unity felt like.

TRIBALISM REPLACED DISCERNMENT

Under Saul, the people split into camps:

- The "Protect Saul at all costs" tribe
- The "This man is unraveling" tribe
- The "We don't want to get involved" tribe
- The "Maybe God will fix this without us" tribe

Division wasn't just political — it was spiritual.

When a leader becomes an idol, people will fracture their own communities to protect him. They will break relationships before they break loyalty to dysfunction.

Friendships strained.

Families argued.

Communities retreated into suspicion.

And the sad truth?

People lost each other long before they lost the battle.

THE NATION COULD NO LONGER AGREE ON WHAT WAS TRUE

Saul's instability created two Israels:

1. **The Israel living in reality**
2. **The Israel living in Saul's narrative**

Saul insisted David was the enemy.

Reality insisted David was faithful.

Saul insisted he was righteous.

Reality insisted he was disobedient.

Saul insisted he heard from God.

Reality insisted he ignored God.

This fracture — between truth and the king's version of truth — tore the nation in half.

Modern readers recognize the pattern instantly:

- One side sees instability.
- The other sees strength.
- One side sees warning signs.
- The other sees persecution.
- One side sees consequences.
- The other sees conspiracy.

When truth becomes optional, unity becomes impossible.

THE EMOTIONAL CLIMATE SHIFTED

Before collapses become visible, the atmosphere changes.

In Israel, you could feel it:

- less trust
- less joy
- less hope
- less confidence
- less clarity

People lived on edge.

They didn't know which version of Saul would show up.

They didn't know which decision would throw the nation into crisis next.

Fear became normal.

Caution became instinct.

Silence became survival.

A divided nation is not one that disagrees — it's one that stops feeling safe.

INTERNAL COLLAPSE ALWAYS PRECEDES EXTERNAL DEFEAT

Israel's greatest battles were not lost on the battlefield.

They were lost in the palace.

When a leader cannot govern himself,

he cannot govern a nation.

Saul's internal chaos became national chaos:

- His insecurity weakened the military.
- His jealousy scattered loyal soldiers.
- His impulsiveness sabotaged victories.
- His paranoia drained morale.
- His erratic decisions destabilized the land.

Israel didn't lose because they lacked weapons.

They lost because they lacked wisdom.

A nation can recover from loss — but not from internal fracture.

THE REMNANT KEPT WATCHING AND WAITING

While the nation argued,

while tribes quarreled,

while loyalists denied the obvious,

while the emotionally exhausted withdrew — **the remnant prayed.**

They didn't have political power.

They didn't have social influence.

They didn't have the numbers.

But they had clarity.

They saw the unraveling not as random chaos,

but as the painful consequence of a choice God had warned them about.

And they held onto one truth:

God had already prepared someone better.

They didn't know David by name yet.

But they knew God would not leave them in this division forever.

Division doesn't begin with conflict.

Division begins with compromise.

- Compromising truth
- Compromising accountability
- Compromising identity
- Compromising righteousness

Israel did not divide because Saul was imperfect.

They divided because Saul was unrepentant — and people were too invested to let go of the fantasy they had built around him.

Chapter 8 teaches us:

- Nations fracture when leaders fracture
- Denial creates tribes
- Pride creates delusion
- Exhaustion creates silence
- Enablers create chaos
- Truth creates separation before it creates unity

And the deepest truth of all:

People rarely see the collapse coming — because they're too busy defending the collapse they're living in.

But even in division, God is already positioning restoration.

Saul's unraveling was not the end.

It was the necessary clearing for David to rise.

THE PERSONAL COST: WHEN LOYALTIES RIP FAMILIES APART

HOW DEVOTION TO A DYSFUNCTIONAL LEADER BREAKS HOMES, HEARTS, AND RELATIONSHIPS

Nations don't divide first on the battlefield or in the voting booth.

They divide at dinner tables.

Under Saul, Israel didn't simply become politically fractured — they became relationally fractured.

Families split.

Friendships strained.

Communities broke into pieces.

People stopped recognizing one another.

It wasn't just a national crisis.

It was a personal one.

Because loyalty to a dysfunctional leader always demands sacrifice — and the first sacrifice is usually the people closest to you.

ISRAEL'S HOMES BECAME HOSTAGE SITUATIONS

Jonathan loved David.

Saul hated him.

Jonathan pursued righteousness.

Saul pursued insecurity.

Jonathan saw truth.

Saul saw threat.

This father-son fracture was not a small disagreement —

it was a spiritual and emotional collision.

Jonathan wasn't rebelling.

He was discerning.

Saul wasn't protecting Israel.

He was protecting his ego.

So the dinner table became a battleground:

- accusations
- shouting
- emotional volatility
- wounded pride
- denial
- rage

Jonathan nearly died simply for aligning himself with God's choice instead of his father's.

That moment set the tone for households across Israel:

"If you don't support the king, you're the problem."

Sound familiar?

When People Choose Loyalty Over Truth, Relationships Become Fragile

In every era of dysfunctional leadership, the same pattern appears:

- siblings stop speaking
- spouses retreat into silence
- cousins delete each other from group chats
- coworkers avoid topics
- church members glare across aisles
- friends quietly drift apart

This isn't politics — it's psychological warfare.

People weren't just defending Saul.

They were defending their identity, their ego, their tribe, their sense of belonging.

And when truth threatens identity, relationships suffer casualties.

The Pain of Watching Someone You Love Descend Into Delusion

Jonathan watched Saul lose himself to paranoia and pride.

He loved his father deeply, but love cannot cure someone who refuses accountability.

This is one of the hardest truths in Scripture:

You can love someone with all your heart and still be unable to save them from their own dysfunction.

Jonathan tried:

- He reasoned
- He mediated
- He interceded
- He spoke truth gently
- He protected David quietly
- He confronted Saul courageously

But Saul wasn't listening.

Not to Jonathan.

Not to Samuel.

Not to God.

Watching someone descend into delusion is one of the most painful experiences a person can endure.

Jonathan experienced that pain on the national stage.

Many people today have experienced the same pain in their own living rooms.

WHEN CONVERSATIONS TURN INTO EMOTIONAL MINEFIELDS

Under Saul, people knew that one wrong sentence could ignite a firestorm.

You could say something truthful and watch a relative explode with defensiveness.

You could point out inconsistencies and suddenly be accused of betrayal.

You could share concerns and be told you "don't understand the bigger picture."

People were walking on relational eggshells — not because truth was unclear, but because denial was loud.

Modern families know this dance well.

It's the tension of loving people who are deeply invested in something that is harming them —

and harming everyone connected to them.

THE RISE OF ALTERNATE REALITIES

Saul didn't just fracture Israel politically.

He fractured their shared understanding of reality.

Some believed David was a threat.

Others knew he was anointed.

Some believed Saul was chosen.

Others saw God had rejected him.

Some believed loyalty meant obedience.

Others believed loyalty meant truth.

Israel wasn't living in one story — they were living in two competing narratives.

Modern society knows this fracture intimately:

- One group sees instability
- Another sees strength
- One sees corruption
- Another sees conspiracy
- One sees consequences
- Another sees persecution

When truth becomes negotiable, unity becomes impossible.

And when unity becomes impossible, relationships become fragile.

WHY FAMILIES BREAK DURING NATIONAL DELUSION

People attach their hopes, fears, and identities to leaders.

They project onto them:

- their insecurities
- their anxieties
- their longing for safety
- their desire for belonging
- their nostalgia for an imagined past

So when you challenge the leader, you're not challenging a political figure — you're challenging their coping mechanism.

This is why arguments felt so personal.

This is why conversations felt so volatile.

This is why logical discussions became emotional explosions.

People weren't defending Saul's behavior.

They were defending the version of themselves that believed following Saul was wise.

THE REMNANT CHOSE TRUTH OVER TRIBALISM

Jonathan stood between two loyalties:

- his father
- and God's plan

He refused to betray righteousness even when pressured by family.

This made him unpopular with Saul but deeply aligned with heaven.

The remnant always makes this choice:

Truth over comfort

Truth over tribe

Truth over loyalty

Truth over ego

Not because they are rebellious but because they refuse to worship a leader.

Jonathan is the patron saint of every:

- adult child who learned to disagree with a parent in love
- spouse who refused to idolize dysfunction
- friend who refused to enable harm
- believer who refused to exalt a political figure above God

The remnant loves truth more than approval.

And that is why they survive seasons of national foolishness.

The collapse of a nation is visible, but the collapse of relationships is felt.

This chapter reveals:

- how denial fractures families
- how loyalty can become idolatry
- how truth can divide before it heals
- how insecurity damages relationships
- how tribalism replaces discernment
- how enabling harms the enabler
- how emotional climates ripple through homes

But the most profound truth:

Jonathan's faithfulness did not save Saul — but it prepared the nation for David.

Sometimes the role of the remnant is not to fix what is broken but to remain grounded until God raises someone who can lead differently.

Jonathan's loyalty to truth, not his loyalty to Saul, helped preserve the spiritual spine of Israel until a better king emerged.

THE IDENTITY CRISIS: WHY THEY STAYED WITH SAUL SO LONG

WHEN A LEADER BECOMES A LIFESTYLE INSTEAD OF A CHOICE

I srael didn't stay loyal to Saul because he was effective.

They stayed because they didn't know who they were without him.

This is the heartbreaking truth about dysfunctional leadership:

People will cling to harmful leaders long after the harm is obvious, because the leader has become part of their identity.

By the time Saul's failures were undeniable, Israel wasn't following a man anymore — they were following a memory, a feeling, a sense of belonging that had quietly wrapped itself around their souls.

Saul wasn't just the king.

He was the narrative they built to make sense of their fear, their insecurity, and their desire for significance.

And letting go of him felt like letting go of themselves.

SAUL WAS THE SYMBOL THEY NEEDED — NOT THE LEADER THEY NEEDED

When Israel asked for a king, they weren't really asking for governance.

They were asking for validation.

They wanted:

- to look strong
- to feel normal
- to fit in with other nations
- to prove they were not "less than"
- to feel secure in a world growing darker

Saul represented all of that.

He was tall.

He was impressive.

He looked decisive.

He looked like the kings other nations admired.

He gave them a sense of collective pride —

even if the substance wasn't there.

People rarely fall in love with leaders.

They fall in love with what the leader represents about *them*.

Saul represented confidence they didn't have, strength they didn't feel, and legitimacy they desperately craved.

That's why they stayed.

THE EMOTIONAL BOND WAS STRONGER THAN THE EVIDENCE

Evidence never changes minds that were formed emotionally.

Logic cannot compete with:

- nostalgia
- fear
- pride
- tribal loyalty
- social belonging
- unspoken insecurities

Once people emotionally attach to a leader, they filter all information through that attachment.

If Saul behaved erratically, they rationalized it.

If Saul disobeyed God, they minimized it.

If Saul threw spears at David, they reframed it.

Their loyalty wasn't blindness.

It was **emotional self-protection.**

Admitting Saul was the wrong choice meant admitting they had misjudged — and that humiliation was harder to face than Saul's behavior.

TRIBAL IDENTITY TOOK PRIORITY OVER SPIRITUAL IDENTITY

Israel had always been God's people.

But under Saul, they slowly became "Saul's people."

This shift was subtle but devastating.

Their righteousness became tied to his reputation.

Their unity became tied to his narrative.

Their self-worth became tied to his success.

And when your identity depends on a leader, you will defend that leader even as he sinks the ship.

People weren't loyal to Saul because he was good.

They were loyal because he represented the tribe they belonged to.

Modern readers know this energy all too well:

- "Us versus them."
- "If you're not with us, you're against us."
- "We don't abandon our own."

It didn't matter if "their own" was wrong.

Tribal belonging outweighed truth.

FEAR LOCKED THEM INTO LOYALTY

Saul's leadership ran on fear — not reverence, not respect, not trust.

Fear of enemies.

Fear of change.

Fear of uncertainty.

Fear of losing status.

Fear of criticism.

Fear of being wrong.

Fear of consequences.

Fear makes people cling to the familiar, even when the familiar is destructive.

Saul's instability was terrifying, but the idea of life *without* Saul was even more terrifying for those who had built their identity around him.

Fear doesn't ask, "Is this wise?"

Fear asks, "Will this keep me safe?"

Even if "safe" is an illusion.

PEOPLE WOULD RATHER SUFFER TOGETHER THAN STAND ALONE IN TRUTH

Jonathan saw the truth early.

The remnant saw it too.

But standing in truth feels lonely,

and standing in a lie feels communal.

People feared isolation more than deception.

So they stayed with Saul

because everyone else stayed with Saul.

This is how nations fall into collective delusion:

Group loyalty requires everyone to pretend at the same time.

Pretend Saul was stable.

Pretend the kingdom was fine.

Pretend David was dangerous.

Pretend Samuel was overreacting.

Pretend things were not collapsing around them.

Shared pretending feels like unity.

Shared deception feels like solidarity.

But truth always breaks the illusion.

THE LONGER PEOPLE DEFEND A BAD DECISION, THE HARDER IT BECOMES TO REVERSE IT

Time strengthens pride.

The more Saul failed, the more the people defended him — because admitting the truth now

meant acknowledging their error then.

People will rewrite entire histories before they rewrite their beliefs.

By the time Saul's reign spiraled beyond denial, people were no longer defending him — they were defending the story they told themselves:

"We chose wisely."

"We meant well."

"We were right."

"We weren't fooled."

When pride hijacks identity, truth feels like personal attack.

That's why they stayed.

WHEN IDENTITY IS BUILT ON A LEADER, COLLAPSE FEELS PERSONAL

The day Israel realized Saul had failed them,

they didn't just feel political disappointment.

They felt humiliation.

They felt confusion.

They felt betrayal.

They felt exposed.

They felt spiritually disoriented.

Losing Saul felt like losing the version of themselves who believed choosing Saul was wise.

This is why the collapse felt so catastrophic:

It wasn't just the nation shaking.

It was their self-image.

And until a nation confronts its identity crisis, it cannot embrace the leader God is raising next.

This chapter exposes a universal spiritual truth:

People don't stay loyal to dysfunction because of the leader.

They stay loyal because of what that leader represents about them.

Chapter 10 teaches us:

- Identity is more powerful than logic
- Loyalty can become bondage
- Fear can masquerade as faithfulness
- Tribalism is emotionally addictive
- Pride resists correction
- Admitting error feels harder than living in it
- People cling to harmful choices when those choices shape their identity

And the most freeing truth:

You can love your past self without letting your past self choose your future.

Israel eventually realized Saul was never their identity.

They were God's people long before Saul, and they remained God's people long after him.

But they had to let the false identity die before the true identity could rise.

And that prepared them for a leader shaped not by insecurity, but by the heart of God.

ACT III

THE CONSEQUENCES THAT BECAME A CLASSROOM

11

WHEN THE CROWN BECOMES A CURSE

THE BLESSING HIDDEN INSIDE CONSEQUENCES

There is a remarkable moment in Israel's story where the symbol that was supposed to bless them the crown begins to feel like a burden they can't put down.

Nobody talks about that part when they romanticize kingship.

People love the idea of a crown.

It shines.

It glitters.

It represents power, prestige, influence, and security.

But a crown on the wrong head becomes something else entirely: **A curse.**

Israel didn't see it at first.

They asked for a king with the enthusiasm of children begging for a new toy:

"We want a king!

We NEED a king!

Other nations have kings!

Why can't WE have a king?

Give us a king right now!"

The crown was supposed to elevate them.

Give them legitimacy.

Boost their confidence.

Make them feel "like everybody else."

But the moment Saul wore it, something shifted:

The crown didn't bless the nation— it began draining it.

It exposed Saul.

It exposed Israel.

It exposed the motives they ignored and the insecurities they carried.

Israel wanted a king to fix their fears.

Instead, the king *revealed* them.

WHEN GOD'S "YES" IS ACTUALLY JUDGMENT

Samuel warned them.

They insisted anyway.

So God did something both gracious and terrifying:

He said yes.

Not because Saul was good.

Not because the timing was right.

But because consequences are sometimes the only teacher stubborn people will listen to.

God didn't choose Saul to *heal* Israel.

He chose Saul to *expose* Israel.

Saul was the mirror they didn't want.

His insecurity reflected their insecurity.

His emotional instability reflected their spiritual instability.

His disobedience reflected their rebellion.

His paranoia reflected their fear.

In choosing Saul, they weren't just choosing a king— they were choosing a revelation of themselves.

Sometimes God gives us what we want so we can finally see what we *need*.

THE COLLAPSE NO ONE SAW COMING — BUT EVERYONE FELT

A nation doesn't crumble in one dramatic moment.

Collapse leaks in like water through tiny cracks.

People started noticing:

- battles not won
- soldiers not inspired
- communities unsettled
- morale slipping
- trust evaporating
- Samuel distancing himself
- David rising behind the scenes

Things felt... off.

But by then, the crown had already turned into a weight.

The symbol of prestige had become an anchor dragging the nation downward.

Israel looked at Saul and saw what they feared to admit:

The king they demanded was dismantling the very nation they wanted him to protect.

This is what happens when expectation collides with reality.

The people asked for glory.

They got dysfunction.

They asked for unity.

They got division.

They asked for pride.

They got embarrassment.

They asked for strength.

They got a man who unraveled under pressure.

And the unraveling didn't just affect the palace — it spread into the soil of the land.

Pain Became the Teacher Israel Had Avoided

By the time consequences became undeniable, Israel had two choices:

1. Keep pretending
2. Or finally tell the truth

Pain has a way of forcing honesty.

The discomfort they avoided in Samuel's warnings became the very discomfort that brought clarity.

Pain taught them what comfort could not.

Pain revealed:

- what pride hid
- what insecurity denied
- what loyalty distorted
- what fear refused to face

Pain is not God's cruelty.

Pain is God's megaphone to people who silence the whisper of wisdom.

Israel didn't change because they were convinced.

They changed because they were confronted.

And consequences did the confronting.

THE BLESSING HIDDEN INSIDE CONSEQUENCES

As terrible as Saul's reign was, it did one holy thing:

It prepared Israel to appreciate David.

If Israel had gotten David first, they would not have understood the gift.

They would have said, "This is fine, but couldn't he be taller?

Flashier?

More exciting?"

But after Saul?

They were DONE with unstable leadership.

DONE with emotional volatility.

DONE with spectacle.

DONE with ego-driven decisions.

DONE with chaos masquerading as strength.

By the time David arrived,

the nation was ready—

not for a celebrity king—

but for a *shepherd*.

Saul created the hunger for what David offered.

His failures became the soil where the next leader's success could grow.

This is the redemptive pattern of God:

Even the consequences of our foolishness can become the foundation for our healing.

A Crown Cannot Change a Character

The tragedy of Saul is not that he wore the crown poorly.

It's that the crown revealed how unprepared he was to carry it.

A position cannot transform what character has not shaped.

Titles do not produce maturity.

Anointing does not override obedience.

Authority does not compensate for insecurity.

Israel wanted a king to give them stability.

But stability cannot be borrowed from a leader — it must be rooted in God.

The crown on Saul's head could not change the cracks in his heart.

And the crown on the wrong head became a national curse.

This chapter teaches us one of the most sobering truths in Scripture:

Sometimes the judgment is not God withholding what we want.

Sometimes the judgment is God letting us have it.

Saul was not a punishment.

He was a revelation.

He revealed:

- the immaturity of the nation
- the fragility of their identity
- the danger of choosing from insecurity
- the cost of ignoring warnings
- the need for godly leadership
- the wisdom of God's timing

And the hope buried inside the collapse was this:

God lets things fall apart only when He is preparing a better leader to rise.

The crown became a curse— but the curse became a doorway to restoration.

12

WAITING FOR A BETTER LEADER: THE LONG PAUSE BEFORE RESTORATION

WHEN GOD HITS THE BRAKES BEFORE MOVING US FORWARD

After the collapse of Saul's reign, Israel entered a strange and uncomfortable season — a divine pause.

It was the space between what had fallen apart and what God was preparing next.

The people weren't in crisis anymore, but they weren't restored either.

This in-between place is where faith matures.

It's also where impatience tries to drag people right back into foolishness.

Israel had learned to recognize chaos, but they had not yet learned to recognize peace.

So God slowed them down.

Because before a better leader could rise, **Israel needed to detox from the one they had chosen.**

THE SILENCE AFTER THE COLLAPSE FELT UNSETTLING

Saul's reign was noisy — full of drama, scandals, emotional outbursts, and panic.

So when he fell, the sudden quiet was jarring.

For the first time in years, the air was still.

But stillness feels foreign to people who've lived inside chaos.

They mistake silence for danger.

They confuse calm with emptiness.

Israel didn't know how to interpret the quiet.

They didn't know if it meant God was distant or if He was drawing them closer.

Sometimes the stillness after a storm is not abandonment — it is the first breath of healing.

GOD WAS NOT RUSHING — HE WAS REBUILDING

Israel was ready to move on quickly.

"Okay, God — Saul is done.

Can we get the next king now?

Preferably someone stable, emotionally mature, handsome, and with a strong military résumé?

David seems nice. Let's expedite this."

But God was not rushing.

He was repairing.

He was softening hearts.

He was reshaping desires.

He was recalibrating identity.

He was preparing the nation to recognize character, not charisma.

Israel wanted a fast solution.

God wanted a lasting transformation.

Before David could rise, the people needed to unlearn everything Saul had taught them:

- that leadership equals spectacle
- that insecurity equals strength
- that noise equals power
- that rebellion equals independence
- that impulsiveness equals courage

God was not just replacing a king — He was reeducating a nation.

THE REMNANT UNDERSTOOD THE PAUSE

While the majority felt restless, the remnant recognized the pause for what it was:

Not delay — preparation.

They knew God never moves slowly without purpose.

The remnant prayed differently:

"Lord, make us ready."

"Lord, heal our land."

"Lord, shape our next leader."

"Lord, cleanse us from what we chose."

"Lord, restore what was broken."

The remnant saw the pause as holy,

not frustrating.

And that awareness positioned them to discern David when others hesitated.

HEALING TAKES TIME — ESPECIALLY AFTER DYSFUNCTION

Saul's leadership had warped Israel's expectations.

They had gotten used to:

- unpredictability
- emotional volatility
- reactive decisions
- spiritual compromise
- fear-based leadership
- tribal loyalty

A healthy leader can't thrive in a nation still addicted to dysfunction.

So God slowed Israel's pace to restore their spiritual reflexes.

He needed them to desire:

- wisdom over excitement
- integrity over entertainment
- obedience over charisma
- humility over spectacle
- righteousness over resonance

God does not place David in a Saul environment until the soil is ready.

Healing was necessary before anointing could be recognized.

WAITING REVEALED THE TRUE CONDITION OF THEIR HEARTS

Waiting exposes motives.

Some Israelites waited with humility.

Others waited with impatience.

Some grew grateful.

Others grew bitter.

Some leaned into God.

Others longed for another Saul.

Waiting always reveals what crisis hides.

In the absence of chaos,

people must face themselves:

- What did we really want in a leader?
- What were we trying to avoid?
- What insecurities drove our choices?
- What warning signs did we ignore?
- Why did we defend dysfunction for so long?

Before restoration, God brings revelation.

And Israel could not receive David until they understood why they chose Saul.

THE PAUSE WAS PROTECTION

If God had rushed the process, Israel would've repeated their mistake.

They would have chosen another Saul — perhaps with different packaging, but with the same internal instability.

God slowed the nation to prevent a relapse.

He was protecting them from:

- desperation-driven decisions
- emotional rebound choices
- repeating generational patterns
- idolizing leadership again
- choosing charisma without character

Sometimes protection looks like delay.

Sometimes mercy sounds like silence.

God paused Israel so He could save Israel.

DAVID WAS ALREADY BEING PREPARED — EVEN IF ISRAEL DIDN'T KNOW IT

While Israel sat in the quiet,

David was in the fields,

learning to lead sheep,

learning to fight lions,

learning to worship alone,

learning to trust God,

learning to steward responsibility.

Israel saw the pause as inactivity.

God saw it as preparation.

The leader they needed was already being shaped by heaven — not in the palace, but in obscurity.

This is God's pattern:

Before He elevates, He equips.

Before He reveals, He refines.

Israel's pause was David's training ground.

This chapter reminds us that God's pace is always intentional.

- The pause is not punishment
- The silence is not abandonment
- The delay is not denial
- The stillness is not stagnation

Sometimes God slows us down so He can rebuild what crumbled under the weight of our own choices.

Saul's collapse was dramatic.

But Israel's restoration was deliberate.

Before David rose, God healed the nation's expectations.

He reshaped their desires.

He refined their discernment.

And He made sure they never again confused charisma for calling, noise for anointing, or spectacle for leadership.

The waiting season was not wasted — it was the womb of a new beginning.

13

THE QUIET RISE OF
A BETTER LEADER

GOD BUILDS IN THE BACKGROUND
BEFORE HE REVEALS IN THE SPOTLIGHT

While Israel was reeling from Saul's instability, God was already crafting the leader who would heal what Saul broke.

But He wasn't doing it in the palace.

He was doing it in obscurity.

The nation was searching for dramatic answers; God was shaping a shepherd.

People wanted a king who looked powerful; God was forming a king who *was* powerful — from the inside out.

This is God's pattern throughout history:

He prepares the solution long before people recognize the problem.

When Israel chose Saul, David was a child.

When Saul spiraled, David was learning faithfulness.

When the nation grew exhausted, David was learning courage.

While people argued, David was learning obedience.

By the time Israel realized they needed a better leader, God had already built one.

DAVID WAS BEING DEVELOPED IN SILENCE

While Saul's reign was loud — full of drama, spectacle, and chaos — David's preparation was quiet.

He wasn't chasing recognition.

He wasn't vying for position.

He wasn't auditioning for the throne.

He was:

- tending sheep
- fighting lions and bears
- practicing music
- mastering slingshot accuracy
- defending the vulnerable
- learning to listen to God
- becoming responsible in private

Nobody saw him.

Nobody celebrated him.

Nobody predicted his rise.

But God saw him.

God celebrated him.

God predicted his rise.

In Saul's world, everything was public and performative.

In David's world, everything was private and purposeful.

One man was unraveling in the palace.

The other was being refined in the pasture.

THE QUALITIES GOD BUILDS BEFORE PROMOTION

David didn't become Israel's next leader because of charisma, beauty, or height — though he had all three.

He became the next leader because he cultivated the traits Saul lacked:

- **Consistency** when nobody was watching
- **Humility** when tempted with pride
- **Courage** without theatrics
- **Obedience** without complaint
- **Tenderness** without weakness
- **Strength** without arrogance
- **Worship** without performance
- **Integrity** without an audience

Saul learned nothing from God's presence.

David lived in it.

This is why God said of David:

"A man after My own heart."

Not "a man after political approval."

Not "a man after public admiration."

Not "a man after the polls."

A man shaped by God's heart becomes a leader shaped by God's wisdom.

ISRAEL NEEDED A LEADER WHO DIDN'T NEED THE THRONE

Saul needed the throne to feel powerful.

David was powerful before he ever sat on the throne.

This is the difference between leadership built on insecurity

and leadership built on identity.

Saul's authority was external — rooted in position, title, and image.

David's authority was internal — rooted in purpose, calling, and character.

The throne didn't build David.

David built the throne.

When God raises someone, the position doesn't define them — they define the position.

THE REMNANT RECOGNIZED DAVID LONG BEFORE THE NATION DID

People trapped in Saul's narrative could not see David clearly at first.

They were used to spectacle.

They were used to emotional volatility.

They were used to leadership as entertainment.

David's quiet steadiness didn't look impressive to those addicted to drama.

But the remnant noticed:

- his humility
- his peace

- his clarity
- his worship
- his obedience
- his lack of ego
- his faith in God

He didn't need to dominate a room.

He didn't need applause.

He didn't need to weaponize fear.

His presence calmed what Saul's presence agitated.

Truth recognizes truth, and wisdom recognizes wisdom.

Those who had stayed faithful to God began to sense:

"This is different.

This is holy.

This is leadership."

DAVID'S RISE WAS NOT ABOUT REPLACING SAUL — IT WAS ABOUT RESTORING ISRAEL

David wasn't a reaction to Saul's failure.

He was the fulfillment of God's intention.

Before Israel begged for a king,

before Saul was crowned,

before the nation spiraled,

before chaos took hold — God had already planned David.

Saul showed Israel what leadership without God becomes.

David showed them what leadership with God can build.

The contrast wasn't accidental.

It was educational.

God wasn't just raising a better king.

He was raising a better nation.

GOD BUILDS CHARACTER BEFORE HE BUILDS INFLUENCE

People often want influence first and character second.

God reverses that order.

David's influence grew because his character was already established.

He didn't crumble under pressure because he had learned to trust God in obscurity.

He didn't break under spiritual weight because he had carried responsibility faithfully in private.

He didn't fear giants because he had faced lions and bears alone.

Public victories are always preceded by private victories.

Israel learned to wait for a leader whose strength wasn't borrowed from the throne but forged in the presence of God.

This is the turning point of the entire book:

It shifts the focus from failure to formation.

From collapse to calling.

From Saul to David.

From human choice to divine preparation.

This chapter teaches us:

- God is building solutions long before we see the need

- Preparation often happens in obscurity
- Character is the foundation of righteous leadership
- Quiet seasons are not wasted seasons
- God refines before He reveals
- True leadership is internal before it is external
- Better leaders rise not from image, but from intimacy with God

And the most beautiful truth:

Saul's failure did not sabotage Israel's future — it positioned them for David's rise.

God wastes nothing, not even our worst choices.

The land was broken, but the leader God was raising would know how to heal it.

A BETTER LEADER RISES

GOD'S ANSWER TO A NATION EXHAUSTED BY FOOLISHNESS

E very season of collapse eventually reaches a point where even the most stubborn hearts whisper:

"There has to be something better than this."

Israel finally reached that moment.

After years of instability, emotional whiplash, broken trust, and national exhaustion, their souls were ready for something steadier — something holy, something whole.

They didn't know the details.

They didn't know God's timeline.

They didn't know David's name yet.

But they knew one thing:

"This... cannot be all God has for us."

And they were right.

God was already moving.

THE RISE OF DAVID WAS NOT A SURPRISE TO GOD — ONLY TO THE PEOPLE

Israel saw a crisis.

God saw a transition.

They saw collapse.

God saw preparation.

They saw the end.

God saw the beginning.

While the nation was unraveling under Saul,

God had been shaping their next leader in the quiet hills of Bethlehem.

David didn't burst onto the scene by accident.

He had been growing in obscurity —

in the fields,

in worship,

in battle,

in solitude,

in surrender.

God had been building the kind of leader Israel didn't even know they needed.

Someone steady.

Someone humble.

Someone courageous.

Someone obedient.

Someone who could carry the weight Saul ran from.

David was heaven's answer to a nation tired of carrying their own dysfunction.

A New Kind of Leadership — One Formed by God, Not Ego

Saul led from insecurity.

David led from identity.

Saul needed applause.

David needed God.

Saul performed strength.

David embodied it.

Saul was driven by fear.

David was driven by faith.

And this is the difference that reshapes nations.

Saul reacted to pressure.

David responded to God.

Saul demanded loyalty.

David cultivated trust.

Saul used the throne to validate himself.

David used the throne to serve the people.

Saul's leadership drained the nation.

David's leadership restored it.

This is why Scripture calls David *"a man after God's own heart"* — not because he was flawless, but because his heart was oriented toward God even when he fell short.

He was the kind of leader whose internal world was strong enough to carry a crown without crushing the nation beneath it.

ISRAEL DIDN'T JUST GET A NEW KING — THEY GOT THEIR BREATH BACK

When David stepped into leadership, something shifted in the atmosphere:

- Hope returned
- Worship returned
- Strategy returned
- Courage returned
- Unity returned
- Wisdom returned

People who had been walking on emotional eggshells could finally exhale.

David didn't govern with theatrics, manipulation, or fear.

He governed with clarity, conviction, and humility.

His presence calmed what Saul's presence agitated.

His leadership healed what Saul's leadership fractured.

His obedience restored what Saul's disobedience damaged.

David reminded Israel of something they had forgotten:

They were God's people.

Not Saul's.

Not fear's.

Not insecurity's.

THE BLESSING HIDDEN IN THE HARD SEASON

Saul's reign had been painful, but it had also been purifying.

By the time David arrived, Israel no longer wanted a flashy king — they wanted a faithful one.

They no longer wanted spectacle — they wanted stability.

They were done with chaos, done with insecurity, done with ego-driven leadership.

Sometimes the blessing of consequences is that they recalibrate our desires so we never choose foolishness again.

Saul had exposed the cracks. David would rebuild the foundation.

GOD ALWAYS HAD A PLAN — EVEN WHEN THE PEOPLE DIDN'T

Israel thought their story was falling apart. God was quietly pulling it together.

They thought they were being punished. God was actually preparing.

They thought the collapse was the end. God knew it was the doorway to something better.

This is the rhythm of redemption:

God lets what is weak fall so He can raise what is strong.

He lets what is unstable crumble so He can establish what is secure.

He lets what is ego-driven break so He can elevate what is Spirit-led.

Saul wasn't the finale.

He was the setup.

And David wasn't the replacement.

He was the restoration.

Chapter 14 is the turning point — the moment hope re-enters the story.

It teaches us:

- God never leaves His people without a path forward
- Collapse is not the end — it is often the clearing
- Consequences can create the hunger for righteousness
- Better leadership begins with better hearts
- God prepares solutions long before we see them
- The next season always has a name, even if we don't know it yet
- Restoration always begins quietly

And this truth anchors everything:

Saul exhausted the nation.

David revived it.

God planned both.

And God was faithful in all of it.

A better leader rises — not because the people deserve it, but because God is merciful.

15

THE SLOW HEALING OF A NATION

HOW RESTORATION ARRIVES GENTLY AFTER YEARS OF CHAOS

Healing rarely arrives with fireworks.

It does not burst through the door shouting, "THE NEW SEASON IS HERE!"

Healing is subtle.

Quiet.

Steady.

Suspiciously gentle.

After the collapse of Saul's reign and the quiet rise of David, Israel entered a season of slow recovery — the kind of healing that sneaks up on you and suddenly makes you realize:

"We're not where we were anymore."

Years of dysfunction had conditioned the people to expect disaster.

So when restoration finally came,

it felt foreign at first.

But God, in His mercy, reintroduced wholeness carefully —

not to overwhelm the nation,

but to retrain its heart.

HEALING BEGINS BEFORE PEOPLE EVEN NOTICE IT

Israel didn't wake up one morning shouting, "We're healed!"

No nation does.

Healing starts in microscopic shifts:

- the air feels lighter
- decisions feel less chaotic
- conversations feel safer
- worship feels sincere again
- leaders stop performing and start listening
- people stop talking about the crisis every five minutes

Healing's first sign is not joy — it's relief.

Israel began to exhale after years of being on edge.

Not with loud celebration, but with small, almost imperceptible sighs of grace.

They didn't yet know how to trust peace, but they were beginning to let it in.

THE PEOPLE NEEDED TIME TO REGAIN THEMSELVES

Trauma doesn't vanish when leadership changes.

Neither does disappointment.

Neither does fear.

Israel had lived through:

- emotional instability
- national confusion
- relational division
- spiritual compromise
- widespread exhaustion

Those wounds didn't evaporate the moment David was anointed.

People still flinched at sudden changes.

Still braced for unpredictability.

Still expected another meltdown.

Still wondered if this stability was too good to last.

That's how trauma behaves: it convinces you to distrust peace.

So God, in His compassion, let the nation relearn:

- what safety feels like
- what purpose feels like
- what unity feels like
- what trust feels like
- what righteousness feels like

Healing is not the removal of pain; it is the restoration of perspective.

REAL HEALING REQUIRES REAL LEADERSHIP

David didn't heal Israel with charisma.

He healed them with consistency.

- He sought God instead of validation

- He unified tribes instead of dividing them
- He strengthened the military instead of weakening it
- He honored the priesthood instead of manipulating it
- He brought worship back to the center instead of ego
- He restored faith instead of feeding fear

Saul made leadership about himself.

David made leadership about God and the people.

The difference was night and day.

The nation felt it immediately — even if it took time for their souls to catch up.

Healing isn't the absence of a bad leader.

Healing is the presence of a righteous one.

WOUNDS BECAME WISDOM

Israel learned more from Saul's reign than they realized.

Pain taught them humility.

Collapse taught them discernment.

Disillusionment taught them clarity.

Turmoil taught them to value peace.

Division taught them the cost of idolatry.

By the time David rose, the people's desires had matured.

They were no longer seduced by image.

They were no longer impressed by theatrics.

They were no longer drawn to instability.

They had become wiser — not because they studied wisdom, but because they survived foolishness.

Some lessons are learned only through fire, and Israel came out refined.

The Nation Slowly Repaired What Saul Had Broken

Under David, restoration wasn't dramatic.

It was systematic.

Israel began rebuilding:

1. **Its identity**
   - They remembered who they were — *God's people first, not the king's people.*
2. **Its worship**
   - David prioritized the presence of God, and the nation followed.
3. **Its unity**
   - Tribes that once argued rediscovered common purpose.
4. **Its courage**
   - Fear dissipated as stability returned.
5. **Its hope**

A steady leader rekindled the belief that God was truly with them again.

A nation heals not through moments, but through rhythms.

David restored healthy rhythms — the kind that reshape a culture from the inside out.

HEALING DIDN'T ERASE THE PAST — IT REDEEMED IT

Israel remembered Saul, but not with bitterness.

Pain had become perspective.

They didn't pretend the chaos didn't happen.

They simply refused to let it define their future.

The scars became reminders: not of failure, but of faithfulness — God's faithfulness, not Saul's.

God had kept them.

God had taught them.

God had preserved them.

God had raised a better leader.

The past no longer controlled them.

It instructed them.

And instruction is always a sign of healing.

This chapter is not about David alone.

It is about what God does in a people who have walked through collapse and survived it.

It teaches us:

- healing is slow and sacred
- God mends before He multiplies
- righteous leadership brings rest
- trauma reshapes expectations
- wisdom often grows in the soil of regret
- hope returns quietly before it returns loudly
- consequences refine the heart

- restoration is a process, not an event

But the most important truth is this:

The God who allows consequences is the same God who sends comfort.

Saul drained the nation.

David revived it.

But God restored it.

And that restoration wasn't rushed — because God is too wise to rebuild a nation faster than He rebuilds its heart.

ACT IV

WHAT GOD WAS DOING THE WHOLE TIME

16

WHEN THE PEOPLE
FINALLY GROW UP

THE SPIRITUAL MATURITY THAT EMERGES
AFTER FOOLISHNESS RUNS ITS COURSE

A nation doesn't mature because it reads a book, attends a seminar, or hears a prophetic warning.

A nation matures when its wounds become wisdom.

By the time David stabilized Israel, the people weren't just recovering — they were growing up.

Something had shifted in them.

Something spiritual.

Something emotional.

Something deep.

They weren't the same people who had begged Samuel for a king "like all the other nations."

They weren't the same crowd who cheered Saul's height like it was a résumé.

They weren't the same insecure community who mistook charisma for calling.

Israel had been refined by consequences and awakened by experience.

And now, finally, they were ready for maturity.

MATURITY BEGINS WITH HONEST REFLECTION

After the dust settled, Israel had to face some hard truths:

- "We didn't choose Saul out of wisdom."
- "We wanted to feel important, not obedient."
- "We ignored Samuel's warnings."
- "We trusted image more than integrity."
- "We overestimated ourselves and underestimated consequences."

This wasn't self-condemnation.

It was self-awareness.

Maturity always begins with the courage to tell the truth — not about others, but about ourselves.

Israel didn't grow up because David showed up.

They grew up because they finally acknowledged how they ended up under Saul in the first place.

Reflection revealed the root.

Truth dismantled the illusion.

Humility opened the door to wisdom.

MATURITY PRODUCES DISCERNMENT

Before Saul, Israel looked at leaders and asked:

"Does he look the part?"

After Saul, they asked:

"Does he honor God?"

"Does he bring peace or chaos?"

"Is he stable?"

"Can he listen?"

"Is he teachable?"

"Does he have a heart aligned with heaven?"

Saul had trained them — painfully — to ask better questions.

People who have survived dysfunction learn to spot it quickly.

They no longer confuse:

- volume with authority
- insecurity with passion
- spectacle with leadership
- ego with strength
- rebellion with boldness
- charisma with calling

Discernment grew in the soil of disappointment.

And Israel finally knew what to look for in a leader — because they had lived with what to avoid.

MATURITY CHANGES APPETITE

Immature people crave spectacle.

Mature people crave substance.

Immature people want to be impressed.

Mature people want to be guided.

Immature people want a king who entertains.

Mature people want a king who obeys God.

After years with Saul, Israel's appetite changed.

They no longer wanted:

- drama
- instability
- constant crises
- unpredictability
- emotional rollercoasters

They wanted peace.

They wanted wisdom.

They wanted integrity.

They wanted the presence of God restored to the center of their national life.

And David provided exactly that — which is why the nation responded to him differently than they ever responded to Saul.

Their souls were finally hungry for what was holy.

MATURITY REJECTS IDOLATRY

One of the most remarkable transformations in Israel was not how they viewed David — but how they no longer viewed leaders.

Under Saul, leadership became idolatry.

Under David, leadership became partnership.

People realized:

"A king is not God.

A king is not a savior.

A king is not the source of our identity."

When Saul fell, their idol fell with him.

When David rose, he refused to let the throne become an idol again.

This combination — a humbled people and a humble leader — healed the nation's relationship with power.

They finally understood:

You can honor leadership without worshiping it.

You can support a leader without surrendering discernment.

This is spiritual maturity.

Maturity Restores Unity

Under Saul, division was the norm.

Under David, unity returned — not because everyone agreed on everything, but because people prioritized righteousness over tribalism.

They remembered they were one nation.

One people.

One covenant community.

One family under God.

Unity didn't mean perfection.

Unity meant shared purpose.

A healed people are harder to divide.

A wise people are harder to manipulate.

A mature people are harder to deceive.

Israel's unity didn't come from David's charisma — it came from their collective resolve to never again let foolishness lead them.

MATURITY ELEVATES WORSHIP

Under Saul, worship was a backdrop — a political accessory used when convenient.

Under David, worship became breath.

It became culture.

It became identity.

He didn't just lead them militarily.

He led them spiritually.

He reminded them that the center of their nation was not the throne — but the presence of God.

A mature people recognize:

- worship is not optional
- obedience is not negotiable
- accountability is not offensive
- God's voice matters more than cultural pressure

Israel's worship deepened

because their discernment deepened.

This is what spiritual adulthood looks like.

MATURITY ALLOWS HEALING TO BECOME TRANSFORMATION

Israel didn't just heal from Saul's reign.

They *changed* because of it.

They became:

- more humble
- more discerning
- more unified
- more grounded
- more spiritually anchored
- more resistant to manipulation
- more aligned with God

Pain had matured them.

Consequences had shaped them.

David had shepherded them.

They were no longer the insecure nation who begged for a king out of comparison.

They had become a nation capable of hosting revival.

This chapter shows us what God ultimately wants:

Not just better leaders — better people.

Not perfect, but perceptive.

Not naive, but discerning.

Not fearful, but faithful.

It teaches:

- Collapse produces clarity
- Mistakes can produce maturity
- Pain can produce wisdom
- God refines people through experience
- Healing prepares the heart for holiness
- Restoration is incomplete without transformation

And here is the truth that ties it all together:

God did not simply raise David to lead the people.

God raised the people to be ready for David.

They grew up — and that growth became the foundation for their next era of peace.

17

THE GOD WHO SAVES A NATION FROM ITSELF

THE MERCY HIDDEN IN JUDGMENT AND THE SOVEREIGNTY BEHIND THE STORY

I f Israel's story teaches us anything, it's this:

God's greatest mercy is not rescuing us from our enemies — it's rescuing us from ourselves.

Saul was not Israel's biggest threat.

Israel's desires were.

Their insecurity.

Their comparison.

Their stubbornness.

Their refusal to listen.

Their longing for what God never ordained.

Saul was simply the mirror reflecting their internal condition.

And when the mirror shattered, Israel finally saw what God had been trying to show them all along:

"Your decisions shape your destiny — but My mercy shapes your future."

ISRAEL NEEDED DISCIPLINE — BUT GOD GAVE DELIVERANCE

People often assume judgment is the opposite of mercy.

It isn't.

Judgment *is* mercy when the alternative is self-destruction.

God didn't abandon Israel to Saul.

He allowed Saul to run his course so the people could outgrow the very desires that led them into bondage.

That's mercy.

He let the consequences confront them, but He never let the consequences consume them.

That's protection.

And the moment their hearts shifted, God shifted the season.

This is the sovereignty of God:

He allows enough discomfort to redirect us, but never enough destruction to destroy us.

GOD DID NOT GIVE THEM SAUL — THEIR HEARTS DID

This part is uncomfortable, but spiritually necessary.

God didn't force Saul on Israel.

He permitted what they insisted on.

He gave them what they wanted so He could position them to desire what they needed.

Saul was not God's ideal; he was God's instruction.

A lived-out parable.

A national sermon.

A consequence with a curriculum.

Saul taught Israel more about their own spiritual weaknesses than a thousand sermons ever could.

When God wants to mature a nation, He doesn't always send comfort.

Sometimes He sends clarity — and clarity often comes wrapped in pain.

God Never Lost Control — Even When the Nation Did

From the outside, Saul's reign looked like chaos.

But behind the scenes, God's hand never left the steering wheel.

He allowed Saul's jealousy, but preserved David's life.

He allowed Saul's instability, but protected the nation from annihilation.

He allowed relational fractures, but raised a remnant who could discern truth.

He allowed national discomfort, but prepared a future king in the shadows.

God didn't cause the chaos — but He wove purpose through every thread of it.

Divine sovereignty does not mean everything is good. It means everything is governed.

Even when it looks like life is spiraling, God is not spiraling with it.

MERCY WAS WORKING EVEN WHEN ISRAEL SAW ONLY CONSEQUENCES

One of the most beautiful themes in Israel's story is that God's mercy was active long before the nation recognized it.

Mercy was present when Samuel warned them.

Mercy was present when they rejected Samuel.

Mercy was present when Saul was anointed.

Mercy was present when Saul failed.

Mercy was present when Saul spiraled.

Mercy was present when the consequences arrived.

And mercy was present when David was preparing in the fields.

God's mercy did not begin with David's rise. It sustained Israel through Saul's fall.

Mercy upheld the nation even when the nation did not uphold God.

GOD PROTECTS DESTINY EVEN WHEN PEOPLE COMPLICATE IT

Israel complicated everything:

- their leadership
- their unity
- their identity
- their worship
- their discernment

But God still protected their destiny.

Saul's dysfunction did not cancel God's covenant.

Israel's stubbornness did not erase God's purpose.

Their misjudgment did not rewrite God's promise.

Human decisions shape the journey,

but divine sovereignty shapes the destination.

People can delay what God intends — but they cannot derail it.

Even in the chaos, God was still guiding history toward David and ultimately toward the Messiah, who would come through David's line.

That is sovereignty.

That is mercy.

That is God.

GOD USES CONSEQUENCES TO BRING CORRECTION — NOT CONDEMNATION

The purpose of consequences is not to destroy people but to develop them.

God used Saul to:

- expose Israel's motives
- purify their desires
- sharpen their discernment
- humble their pride
- restore their dependence
- recalibrate their expectations
- prepare them for David

Consequences were not God's anger.

They were God's correction.

And correction is always an act of love.

Because the God who disciplines is the same God who delivers.

THE NATION THAT CHOSE WRONG BECAME THE NATION GOD CHOSE AGAIN

Here is the redemptive twist:

The same people who demanded Saul became the people God entrusted with David.

Their failure did not disqualify them.

It positioned them.

Their collapse did not end their story.

It rewrote it.

Their mistakes did not define them.

God's mercy did.

Israel is proof that:

- God restores what we ruin
- God rebuilds what pride breaks
- God redirects what rebellion misguides
- God rescues us from cycles we cannot break alone

The nation that fell under Saul rose under David because God's mercy remained stronger

than their worst choices.

This reveals the theological heart of your book:

God's sovereignty does not erase human responsibility, but human failure does not erase God's mercy.

This chapter teaches:

- God gives us agency — but He governs outcomes
- Consequences refine us — but mercy restores us
- Judgment wakes us — but grace heals us
- Stubbornness delays blessing — but does not destroy God's plan
- God works through the collapse — not just the victory
- Redemption is always bigger than failure
- God saves nations from the leaders they choose AND from the desires that led them there

And the deepest comfort:

God never abandons His people —

not in their disobedience,

not in their consequences,

not in their confusion,

not in their collapse.

Israel chose Saul, but God chose Israel. And God's choice always wins.

WHEN A NATION FINALLY BREATHES AGAIN

THE RESTORATION OF CLARITY, COMMUNITY, AND COURAGE AFTER CHAOS

There comes a moment — often quiet, often small — when a nation that has lived through chaos suddenly notices something it hasn't felt in years:

Peace.

Not the loud, dramatic kind.

Not the shallow "everything is fine" kind.

But the deep, internal kind that settles the shoulders, softens the breath, and whispers:

"We made it through."

After surviving Saul's dysfunction, Israel entered a season of recovery that felt almost unreal.

For the first time in a long time,

they weren't waiting for the next crisis.

They weren't holding their breath.

They weren't bracing for emotional whiplash.

They weren't tiptoeing around instability.

They were simply… living.

And living felt holy again.

PEACE FEELS STRANGE WHEN YOU'RE USED TO SURVIVING

When people have lived through a long season of chaos, the calm can feel suspicious.

Israel kept looking around, waiting for something to go wrong.

- "Is this stability real?"
- "Is this joy allowed?"
- "Is this unity sustainable?"
- "Is this calm just the setup before the next storm?"

That's what trauma does — it trains the heart to mistrust good things.

But slowly, gently, quietly, Israel relearned peace:

- conversations without tension
- decisions without drama
- worship without hypocrisy
- leadership without fear
- families without division
- daily life without exhaustion

Peace stopped feeling foreign and started feeling familiar.

Healing starts when peace feels possible again.

CLARITY RETURNED FIRST

Under Saul, truth was foggy.

Facts were flexible.

Reality was negotiable.

Discernment was drowned out by spectacle.

When David took the throne, clarity returned in layers:

- motives became clear
- truth became visible
- consequences made sense
- the past felt understandable
- the future felt hopeful

Clarity is a sign of restoration. It means the soul is no longer spinning.

Israel could finally see:

- where they went wrong
- what they had learned
- who they had become
- and how God preserved them

Clarity is the gift that comes after confusion has exhausted its power.

THEN COMMUNITY RETURNED

Saul's reign scattered people emotionally and spiritually.

People withdrew to protect their hearts.

Families argued.

Tribes drifted.

Suspicion flourished.

Division became normal.

But under David, community blossomed again.

People started opening their doors, their hands, their hearts.

Neighbors stopped looking at each other as representatives of rival tribes and started seeing each other as fellow Israelites again.

David's leadership restored what Saul's fear had eroded:

- belonging
- generosity
- unity
- shared purpose

This wasn't political unity.

It was relational unity.

The kind that rebuilds the social fabric of a nation.

COURAGE RETURNED NEXT

Saul governed with insecurity, and insecurity always breeds fear.

Under David, courage resurfaced.

Israel began to dream again.

To build again.

To strategize again.

To fight with purpose again.

To worship with confidence again.

Fear receded as stability grew.

People stopped living from reaction and started living from intention.

This is what righteous leadership does — it doesn't just restore order. It restores courage.

GRATITUDE BECAME THE NEW RHYTHM

After years of drama, the absence of chaos becomes something sacred.

Israel became grateful for things they once took for granted:

- predictable days
- wise decisions
- spiritual integrity
- national purpose
- relational safety

Gratitude always follows deliverance.

Not because everything becomes perfect, but because the people recognize how far God has carried them.

They remembered the years of confusion. And they thanked God for the clarity.

They remembered the battles of insecurity. And they thanked God for the confidence.

They remembered the wounds. And they thanked God for the healing.

Gratitude is the fruit of survival.

GOD'S FAITHFULNESS BECAME THE STORY

At the end of it all, Israel saw a truth they couldn't see in the middle of the chaos:

God had been faithful the entire time.

Faithful in warning them.

Faithful in letting them choose.

Faithful in letting consequences teach.

Faithful in preserving the remnant.

Faithful in shaping David.

Faithful in restoring the nation.

Faithful in turning their sorrow into wisdom.

Faithful in turning their regret into discernment.

Saul's season had been painful, but God's presence had never left.

Every tear became testimony.

Every mistake became instruction.

Every wound became wisdom.

Every detour became direction.

God had carried Israel from disillusionment

to discipline

to deliverance

to discernment

to destiny.

This is the breath after the storm — the moment the nation realizes God didn't just rescue them.

He **renewed** them.

He **restored** them.

He **reset** them.

He **reclaimed** them.

It teaches us:

- Peace is a sign of God's presence
- Clarity is a sign of God's mercy
- Unity is a sign of God's healing
- Courage is a sign of God's restoration
- Gratitude is a sign of God's maturity
- Survival is evidence of God's sovereignty

And the most comforting truth:

A nation can survive the collapse of a leader when the hand of God is still holding it together.

Israel breathed again — not because David was perfect, but because God was faithful.

And God always is.

19

WHEN GOD REWRITES THE STORY

THE REMNANT'S FAITH, GOD'S TIMING, AND THE DAWN OF A NEW ERA

E very season of collapse eventually reaches a turning point — the sacred moment when brokenness becomes clarity and clarity becomes hunger for something better.

Israel finally reached that moment.

After the noise, after the chaos, after the wounds, and after the long exhaustion of Saul's reign, a quiet truth began to settle across the land:

"We cannot stay here."

The nation had been humbled.

The remnant had been praying.

The people had grown wiser.

And heaven had been moving long before the people realized it.

Israel didn't know the details.

They didn't know the timing.

They didn't see the full unfolding.

But God did.

And in His sovereignty, He began lifting a leader whose presence would break the cycle

their choices had created.

COLLAPSE IS NEVER THE END — IT'S THE CLEARING

Saul's failure felt catastrophic, but heaven saw it differently.

What looked like the end to Israel was the clearing God needed for restoration.

Before God plants something new, He often removes what cannot sustain the next season.

Saul's instability had run its course.

His ego had exhausted the nation.

His decisions had exposed the weakness of image-driven leadership.

His insecurities had fractured unity and drained national courage.

And now the ground was finally soft enough for God to plant something righteous.

This is why collapse, as painful as it is, can also be mercy in disguise.

It makes room for what we should have wanted all along.

The Remnant Stood in the Gap, Holding the Line in Prayer

While the nation struggled, the remnant carried the assignment nobody applauds in the moment:

Intercession.

They prayed when others panicked.

They stayed faithful when others fractured.

They looked to God when others looked to the throne.

They held their spiritual ground

long enough for the nation to survive its own decisions.

The remnant did not overthrow Saul.

They didn't lead protests.

They didn't organize rebellions.

They simply remained steady — refusing to surrender their discernment even when surrounded by denial.

Their prayers became the spiritual backbone that kept Israel from total collapse.

They didn't create David, but they created the atmosphere David would eventually walk into.

God Was Preparing the Leader Long Before the Nation Was Ready

While Saul spiraled publicly, David was being shaped privately.

God was not reacting to Israel's crisis — He was already writing the solution.

In the fields,

David was learning courage.

Learning responsibility.

Learning worship.

Learning obedience.

Learning to trust the unseen God

instead of the unstable structures around him.

David wasn't waiting for a throne; he was becoming the kind of man who could carry one without corrupting his soul.

Israel didn't know his name yet, but God was stitching their future into the fabric of David's formation.

This is the beauty of divine timing:

God prepares the answer before people even understand the question.

THE NATION FINALLY DESIRED WHAT GOD ALWAYS INTENDED

After living through Saul's reign, Israel's appetite changed.

They were done with:

- spectacle
- volatility
- ego-driven decrees
- insecurity disguised as strength
- chaos masquerading as courage
- leadership that felt like emotional turbulence

They were ready for:

- peace
- wisdom
- stability
- humility
- unity
- righteousness

They were ready for a leader whose strength wasn't rooted in image but in intimacy with God.

What had once impressed them now exhausted them.

What had once intimidated them now embarrassed them.

What had once captivated them now convicted them.

The people who once demanded Saul were now prepared to receive David.

THE BETTER LEADER DIDN'T JUST RISE — HE REVEALED GOD'S HEART

David's rise wasn't about political restoration.

It was about spiritual recalibration.

He reminded Israel of what they had forgotten:

- God was their true King
- The throne serves God's purposes, not personal ego
- Leadership is stewardship, not performance
- Identity comes from God, not from hierarchy
- Unity comes from righteousness, not rhetoric

David didn't lead with insecurity.

He led with worship.

He didn't lead with paranoia.

He led with confidence in God.

He didn't lead by dominating the people.

He led by serving them.

He didn't lead to impress the nations.

He led to honor the God who raised him.

Through David, Israel encountered a truth:

God does not just fix crises. He replaces foundations.

THE CYCLES THAT BOUND THE NATION WERE BROKEN

The cycle of:

- insecurity
- emotional chaos
- reactionary leadership
- tribal division
- spiritual compromise

came to an end.

Not because Israel suddenly became perfect, but because their desires finally aligned with God's desires.

Saul taught them what they should never return to.

David showed them what was possible when obedience becomes the anchor of leadership.

And the nation that once chose foolishly now walked in wisdom because they had learned —

painfully — what foolishness feels like.

This is the culmination of the book's central truth:

God never leaves His people in cycles they are willing to outgrow.

It teaches us:

- Collapse creates clarity
- Clarity creates hunger
- Hunger creates readiness
- Readiness creates transformation
- The remnant sustains a nation until its wisdom matures

- God prepares leaders long before we know their names
- Divine timing cannot be rushed
- Restoration is always God's specialty

And the most hopeful truth:

A better leader rises not because the people deserve him, but because God is faithful even when the people are not.

The story didn't end with Saul's chaos.

It ended with God's mercy — embodied through a leader He had crafted with His own hands.

20

WHEN THE STORY COMES FULL CIRCLE

HOW GOD REDEEMS CHOICES, REBUILDS NATIONS, AND RESTORES WHAT FOOLISHNESS TRIED TO DESTROY

There is a moment in every God-written story when the threads that once looked tangled suddenly reveal a pattern.

A moment when confusion gives way to clarity.

A moment when regret becomes revelation.

Israel reached that moment.

Not when Saul fell.

Not when David rose.

But when the nation finally understood:

"God was writing a story bigger than our choices."

For the first time in years, the people could look back at the chaos, the collapse, the consequences, and the slow rebuilding — and see the faithfulness of God woven through every chapter.

They had lived through the regret.

They had survived the fallout.

They had endured the consequences.

They had matured through the pain.

And now, standing on the other side, they could finally breathe the truth:

"God never abandoned us. Even when we abandoned wisdom."

GOD DIDN'T JUST REPLACE A LEADER — HE REWROTE A NATION'S HEART

It would be easy to think the story is simply about a bad king being replaced by a better one.

But God was doing far more than political restructuring.

He was restoring:

- their identity
- their discernment
- their unity
- their worship
- their courage
- their spiritual backbone

Saul didn't just fail as a leader.

Saul revealed the cracks in Israel's heart.

And David didn't just succeed as a leader.

David revealed the healing God had done in them.

This is the mercy of God:

He doesn't just fix what we broke. He transforms us so we don't break it the same way again.

PAIN PREPARED THEM FOR WISDOM

Israel's journey had come full circle, but they were not the same people who begged Samuel for a king "like all the other nations."

They had become:

- wiser
- more humble
- more discerning
- more united
- more spiritually grounded

Pain had done its work. Consequences had taught their lessons. Survival had shaped their souls.

They no longer chased image.

They no longer worshiped charisma.

They no longer mistook ego for leadership.

The same nation that once chose Saul out of insecurity was now choosing obedience out of maturity.

That is transformation.

That is spiritual growth.

That is redemption.

DAVID'S RISE WAS THE BEGINNING, NOT THE ENDING

Many people assume the story climaxes when David becomes king. But biblically, that moment isn't the finish line — it's the reset button.

David's rise marked the beginning of:

- restored worship
- righteous governance
- national unity
- military stability
- spiritual renewal
- cultural identity
- generational blessing

Saul's reign had taken Israel off the path.

David's reign placed them back on it.

One leader drained the nation.

The other revived it.

But both were allowed by God to shape the nation into the people He intended them to be.

This is the sovereignty of God in full display:

He uses both our mistakes and our miracles to move us toward destiny.

THE REMNANT'S ROLE WAS FINALLY SEEN

Throughout Saul's dysfunctional reign, the remnant prayed quietly. They stood firm. They refused to surrender to emotional chaos. They held the nation in intercession when nobody noticed.

But now — in the light of David's leadership — their influence became visible.

Their faithfulness had not been wasted.

Their hope had not been foolish.

Their prayers had not been ignored.

They had been preparing the spiritual atmosphere for the very leader God was raising.

This is how God works:

The remnant builds the runway before the plane ever appears on the horizon.

GOD'S REDEMPTION IS BIGGER THAN ISRAEL'S REGRET

By the time David sat on the throne, Israel realized something profound:

Their regret was real — but God's redemption was greater.

Their failure wasn't final.

Their choices weren't fatal.

Their story wasn't over.

God had taken:

- their stubbornness
- their shortsightedness
- their insecurity
- their idolatry
- their disobedience

and turned all of it into the soil that would grow wisdom, unity, and strength.

Nothing was wasted.

Not even their worst decisions.

This is the God who can take the ashes of a nation and build a testimony out of it.

WHEN THE STORY COMES FULL CIRCLE, GLORY GOES TO GOD ALONE

By the time Israel was restored, no one could take credit for the turn-around except God.

Not Samuel.

Not David.

Not the elders.

Not the tribes.

Not the soldiers.

Not the system.

God had orchestrated the warning.

God had allowed the consequence.

God had preserved the remnant.

God had shaped the new leader.

God had restored the nation.

He didn't just redeem the story.

He authored it.

And the people finally saw:

"We asked for a king to save us. But it was God who saved us from the king we asked for."

This is the hinge that swings you to clarity and hope.

It teaches that:

- A nation can survive its worst decisions
- Collapse can become catalyst

- Regret can become revelation
- Consequences can become curriculum
- Remnants can sustain nations
- God restores what foolishness damages
- The story is never as broken as it feels
- Divine sovereignty is working even when human wisdom is not

And the truth that closes this chapter:

A better leader rose — not because Israel got everything right, but because God kept everything sovereign.

The story ends with David, but it was always about God.

THE LESSON WE WERE
NEVER SUPPOSED TO MISS

HOW GOD USES REGRET,
REBELLION, AND REDEMPTION
TO REWRITE A NATION'S STORY

E very story in Scripture carries a lesson, but some lessons are so costly that God makes sure we never forget them.

Israel's journey through Saul's reign wasn't recorded so we could shake our heads at ancient foolishness. It was recorded so we could recognize our own.

Because at its core, this story is not about kings at all.

It is about **human hearts** and the way we choose leaders when fear is loud and wisdom is quiet.

It is about what happens when desire outruns discernment.

It is about what happens when insecurity becomes decision-making strategy.

It is about what happens when people choose image over integrity, charisma over character,

and familiarity over faithfulness.

It is about us —

every generation,

every nation,

every heart that has ever whispered:

"Give us what we want now."

And the God who answers, not because the request is wise, but because the lesson is necessary.

The Real Story Was Never Saul — It Was Israel

Saul was the surface problem.

Israel's desires were the root.

They wanted a king because they forgot they already had One.

They wanted a crown because they thought a symbol could heal insecurity.

They wanted to look like other nations because they forgot they were called to be different.

Saul wasn't the beginning of the problem — he was the evidence of it.

And God, in His mercy, allowed the evidence to run its course until the people saw with painful clarity what happens when they trust their impulses more than God's instruction.

But God Did Not Leave Them in Their Regret

Even at their worst, Israel's story did not end with judgment.

It ended with **mercy**.

Mercy that preserved the remnant.

Mercy that shaped David in obscurity.

Mercy that redirected a nation without erasing it.

Mercy that rebuilt what rebellion had broken.

Because this is who God is:

He lets consequences teach, but He never lets consequences define.

He lets foolishness run its course, but He never lets foolishness have the final word.

He lets nations feel the weight of their choices, but He never abandons them to those choices.

Regret may be the classroom — but redemption is always the graduation.

THE LESSON FOR US TODAY

This story is not ancient history.

It is a mirror.

We are still capable of choosing Sauls.

We are still capable of defending dysfunction.

We are still capable of worshiping image.

We are still capable of confusing noise with leadership.

We are still capable of loving the idea of strength instead of the substance of it.

And God still allows us to feel the consequences of misplaced trust.

Not to punish us — but to mature us.

Not to shame us — but to shape us.

Not to destroy us — but to deliver us.

Every generation faces its own version of Saul.

And every generation is offered the same invitation:

Grow wiser.

Grow humbler.

Grow discerning.

Grow faithful.

Because God always has a David in development — but He also wants a people prepared to receive him.

THE GOD WHO WRITES THE ENDING

If Israel's story teaches anything,

it is this:

God is more faithful than we are foolish.

He is more committed to our destiny than we are to our detours.

He is more invested in our future than we are in our regrets.

And He is more skilled at writing redemption than we are at writing disaster.

Saul was not the end of Israel's story.

And your Sauls — whether personal, relational, political, or spiritual — are not the end of yours.

God is still the Author.

God is still sovereign.

God is still merciful.

God is still patient.

God is still rewriting what you thought was ruined.

The nation survived its worst decisions.

So will you.

The nation found hope again.

So will you.

Because the same God who preserved Israel preserves you.

He does not abandon His people —

not in rebellion,

not in regret,

not in consequences,

not in collapse.

The story ends with restoration because God wrote it that way.

And He is still writing.

AFTERWORD

THERE IS A MOMENT

WHEN DESIRE BECOMES DEMAND—AND CONSEQUENCES FOLLOW.

Y'all Wanted a King explores one of the most honest and uncomfortable truths in Scripture:

sometimes what we ask God for is not what we need—but what reveals us.

Israel wanted a king.

They demanded one.

And God let them have it.

Not as a blessing—but as a lesson.

This book is not just a biblical commentary on leadership gone wrong. It is an invitation to examine how often we chase visibility over wisdom, control over trust, and familiarity over discernment. It asks us to sit with our own choices—and to notice how faithfully God shows up, even when we insist on learning the hard way.

As an author, I value your perspective deeply. Your review is more than feedback—it is a conversation.

When you share your thoughts on Amazon, you help other readers who are wrestling with leadership, faith, disappointment, and discernment find a book that names what they've been feeling but couldn't quite articulate.

Your words help this message reach people who are standing at the same crossroads—wondering whether what they want is actually what will serve them.

THANK YOU FOR READING.

THANK YOU FOR REFLECTING.

THANK YOU FOR SHARING YOUR VOICE.